SOARING FOR DIAMONDS

Flying for the Highest International Soaring Emblem

Cirro-Q

SOARING FOR DIAMONDS

BY JOSEPH COLVILLE LINCOLN

NORTHLAND PRESS, FLAGSTAFF, ARIZONA

TO DON BARNARD
WHO TAUGHT ME HOW TO SOAR

Foreword

"As far back as any one can go in history, it appears that man has looked at the wide expanse of air above him with longing, and at the birds and insects, sole natural conquerors and utilizers of this realm, with envy."

So wrote Captain Ralph S. Barnaby in his *Gliders and Gliding,* one of the first books published in this country on the sport of soaring.

Three decades after Barnaby's treatise which covered the beginnings of the sport of flying without power, we come to Joseph C. Lincoln's document of experiences and adventures.

During this relatively short period, the art, sport, and science of motorless flying has advanced enormously. Despite this advancement, there has been little authoritative writing on this subject by American soaring pilots. Yet through the years these pilots have been among the world's greatest exponents of the art, both from the standpoint of machine design and operating skill. Today, American pilots hold a preponderance of the world soaring records and claim credit for the creation of many highly refined soaring aircraft.

Although soaring is reasonably available to almost anyone, relatively few people in the United States have much knowledge of it. Here, in Mr. Lincoln's personal accounts, anyone may vicariously experience one of the world's most sophisticated sports. Here is man's very closest approach to the free, quiet, and unfettered flight of nature's most graceful creatures — the birds. It provides, as nothing else, a sense of loneness, a fulfillment of grace and beauty, fun, and that rarest of jewels — inner satisfaction.

E. J. Reeves

Acknowledgements

I would like to express my thanks to Paul F. Bikle, William H. Coverdale, Graham Thomson and E. J. Reeves for the great encouragement they have given this project. For actual help in the work I am indebted to George W. Lauman, Dorothy Payne, Frederic S. Marquardt, Dr. Collice Portnoff, John P. Frank, Desmond Muirhead, and Mary C. Flynn.

Although soaring is much more widely practiced in Europe than in America, (there are over 30,000 soaring pilots in Germany alone; an estimated 150,000 on earth); as of March, 1967, there were only 509 Diamond pilots in the world, of whom 66 were from the United States.

This book is the tale of a series of flights leading up to one Diamond C.

Joseph C. Lincoln

Contents

Illustrations

First Flight

My first ride in a sailplane was on February 19, 1956, at Falcon Field near Mesa, Arizona. It was chilly and my leather jacket felt good. It was also a perfect day for soaring, but I did not know it.

Any sailpilot would immediately have seen the wonderful cumulus clouds with their good vertical development and even spacing. He would have been exalted because it was the beginning of a new season after the long dead period of November, December, and January. He would have known you could stay aloft in that morning sky for hours without any trouble, and could have given a fairly accurate estimate of cloudbase altitude which was 5100 feet above terrain that day; he probably would have noted the hole in cloud cover to the northwest —an area to be avoided on any cross-country flight.

Soaring

I was a power pilot. During the last eight years I had flown three quarters of a thousand hours from one coast to the other and had kept my aircraft away from dangerous weather. My knowledge of meteorology was a knowledge of what to stay out of. To me the sky condition that day was "scattered."

As I arrived at the field that day for my first instruction, a gigantic white sailplane was on tow. We watched as it was pulled up into the sky behind a Piper Super-Cub at the end of a long rope which connected the two aircraft. Later, I found out the sailplane was a Schweizer TG-3 and to my unsophisticated eye it looked like a flying locomotive. The Super-Cub towplane struggled higher and higher for an interminable period.

"He's cut," somebody finally said. Three seconds later the engine's laboring roar was replaced by the sound of idling. I could just hear the whistle of air passing over the Super-Cub as it went into a dive and maneuvered for a landing at the far end of the field. His approach was so badly planned it soon became obvious the pilot would have to go around for another try at his landing; then as the Piper neared our end of the field about 150 feet high, the towrope was dropped, and I realized this pattern was intentional. The pilot made a 180 degree turn, flew a downwind leg, turned on base, final, and landed, stopping the engine before he had even rolled into his parking position. He knew what he was doing.

In the sudden quiet there was the sound of gentle west wind and the sound of excited talking from the people who watched the sailplane circle in a thermal and soar upward rapidly. Great cloudshadows moved over the slopes of nearby McDowell Peak and Sawik Peak and Scarface Mountain, which later stood out again.

Thinking back to childhood, I had always wondered why soaring was not popular in Arizona. One day when

I was a boy my father had taken my brother and sister and me on a picnic. We climbed to the top of Camelback Mountain and ate there, enjoying the view and watching buzzards work slope lift on the cliff which faces northward. A piece of wax paper from one of the sandwiches had not been folded and presently a rising bubble of air which is called a thermal came by, swept it out over the cliff, and carried it aloft. For a long time we watched it, getting smaller and smaller with the great height, until it gave the illusion of trembling in the air. On another occasion there was a schoolmate who lost a small powered model airplane in a thermal. It must have accidentally established a turn which kept it in lift because it went so high that he could no longer follow it even with binoculars. It was found several days later, undamaged.

In Arizona, several previous efforts to get soaring started had come and gone. The spark of interest was turned into a flame in 1955 when Don Barnard came over from California. He crystallized local interest, became one of the founders of the Arizona Soaring Association and its chief instructor. Weekends and some weekdays he was out at the airport—deeply tanned, slender as Mahatma Ghandi, with the face and moustache of a British Air Force Officer, deep musical voice; he was everything in soaring: teacher, disciplinarian, humorist, errand runner, poet, and pilot.

I had seen him a number of times through the autumn and winter and now he introduced me to the others who were gathered near the towplane and sailplanes which were parked in a row beside one end of the strip. A tan sailplane with a red and white striped rudder indicating it was war surplus now waited, broadside to the wind. Someone told me it was an LK which stood for Laister-Kaufman, and its wingtip near the wind lay on the ground and was weighted down by a parachute.

After a few minutes, the scene came to life. The sailplane was wheeled out on the line and Don Barnard buckled on a parachute. Another man helped Margy Crowl, a new student, into hers. Both Don and Margy wore flight suits. Then, with quite some discussion and huffing and puffing she climbed into the front seat and had the shoulder harness and seat belt adjusted and fastened. Don got into the back. Safety belts were put on, the canopies were pulled down and secured, and the wingtip resting on the ground was held up level by a tip-runner, indicating to the tow-pilot the sailplane was ready.

At the other end of the line the Super-Cub had been cranked up and taxied out. The man who had swung the propeller now connected the forward end of the towrope to a hitch below the rudder of the plane and signalled the pilot to creep forward slowly to draw slack out of the line. When it was taut the pilot put his head out the side window and looked back at the sailplane. He saw the wing held level, pulled his head back in and closed the window. Then he pulled on one notch of flap to increase the climbing speed of the towplane and gradually opened the throttle. As they moved forward on tow the wingman held the tip level for a hundred feet by which time he was at a dead run and the pilot in the sailplane had aileron control. The wing staggered momentarily and we could see full control movements of the rudder and ailerons, then the ship levelled and presently it lifted off the runway.

Their flight was a brief one during which no soaring was attempted. After release, two thousand feet above ground, the sailplane was put through the usual maneuvers given to students. When they were down to 500 feet a landing pattern was set up. We watched them fly downwind; then turn smoothly on base leg, turn again on final approach, settle to the ground, bounce just a little and roll up to where we were standing. Don Barnard got out. He

4

MILLIE NOBLES

LK-10A

took off his parachute and crouched low beside Margy Crowl in the front seat. For perhaps two minutes he talked to her, quietly and earnestly, and answered several questions. These were last minute instructions before a first solo.

Then he reached back inside the plexiglass to fasten the rear canopy; the front canopy was pulled over her head and fastened, the towrope was connected again, and she gave the order to raise the wingtip. Half a minute later she was moving down the runway, and then quite suddenly she was airborne on her first solo. After releasing at 2000 feet, she found no lift and her flight was very short, but the landing was excellent, and she was congratulated by all who were present.

Another instruction flight went off and then came my turn. First there was the parachute business. I had not worn one since I was a student going after a private license more than eight years before, and even then it was only for instruction in spins and for the check ride. A good deal of adjustment was necessary on the straps, but in due course I was buckled in. Don quickly told me how to leave the sailplane and open the parachute if anything went wrong. Then I started getting into the seat.

I confess I had smiled a little at seeing Margy get in, but now it was my turn to supply the laughs. In such a narrow space the parachute made me very awkward, and I could not seem to figure out how to get the parachute and my legs in at the same time. If one went in the other did not have enough room. On the third undignified try, I made it and then discovered I was sitting on the seat belt.

The wingman is the Jack of all trades who connects the towrope, checks tow release, runs the wingtip and helps pilots into the parachute and cockpit. He was standing right beside me and while I used both arms to raise myself, he retrieved the hiding belt and brought the shoulder harness around on either side of my neck. He showed me how to connect them. It was my first experience with a shoulder harness and it felt very strange. The belts were tightened, and I was ready to go. The wingman swung the canopy over my head, and I reached and fastened it down. Then he pointed out the towline release knob, and the handle which controls the spoilers and brake. Meanwhile, Don was getting in behind me, but I could not see much because the shoulder harness kept me from turning.

The towrope was connected and the wingman asked me to check the release. I pulled the knob; the steel eye at one end of the rope fell off, and was then reconnected for the actual tow. All the while it was like being in a sailboat heeling in the wind because the left wingtip was on the ground.

I looked at the surprisingly complex instrument panel and set the clock on high noon so it would record the duration of my flight. The one indispensable instrument for soaring flight is the variometer, a highly sensitive rate-of-climb indicator which approaches instantaneous reaction speed. Unlike those of soaring birds, human senses are not acute enough to judge climb with sufficient rapidity for more than very crude soaring. The variometer makes up for this deficiency. Next in order of importance is the airspeed indicator which helps a pilot control speed in the sensitive area just above the stall when he is circling, or "thermalling," to gain altitude. The altimeter, a standard barometric aircraft instrument for giving height information, is third in importance.

"Raise the wing," Don shouted.

The wingtip runner lifted the tip three feet off the ground, levelling the sailplane. Ahead, the Super-Cub crawled forward until the towline was straight. We could see the pilot's head come out of the window momentarily, then disappear. His flaps came down one notch; the idling propeller speeded up into a blur, and then we began to roll.

The wheel on Don's LK made an unmusical scraping noise with each revolution and we heard the scrapes rapidly accelerate. In a moment, the sailplane left ground and the wheel began turning more slowly. Now there was loud airnoise, the banging of control cables, and a remarkable collection of honks, tweets, and peeps, as if the ship were an asthmatic pipe organ. This was quite a shock to one who had been propagandized on the beautiful silence of motorless flight.

"You get her up ten or fifteen feet, then give enough forward stick pressure to let her gradually sink toward the ground. That lets the drag off the towplane so it can take off," Don shouted.

When we were back down within about six feet of the ground the towplane lifted off. The nylon towrope connecting the two planes was a hundred yards long and had a gentle sag in the middle.

"Now pull up with the stick so you stay just a little above him. Don't overcontrol. That's better. Yaw a little if you get slack in the rope. When the towplane turns, keep your nose pointed at his outer wingtip. Otherwise you will turn inside of his path and slack the rope."

The whole process felt awkward in the extreme, and it was remarkable to be within a hundred yards of a flying aircraft and not hear its engine. I now concentrated on holding correct position behind the towship and the minutes went by as we got higher. It seemed a long time because I was anxious to be at last in free flight; I had wondered what it was like for a good part of thirty years.

The beginning was already here. Ahead there was no spinning propeller at the nose; we looked out through a very long, flatly inclined plexiglass windshield which had ripples of distortion toward the front where it joined the

8

blue decking forward of the instrument panel. In the panel itself, there were no engine instruments, and there were two variometers.

Off to the side of us now and far above was the giant white sailplane, lazily pulling up into a series of stalls. It was a beautiful maneuver in which the nose was pulled far above the horizon until flying speed was lost, then the nose fell through the horizon and the aircraft went into a shallow dive until flying speed was regained.

"You tap the panel to get the lag out of your altimeter," Don shouted. I tapped it with my fingertips and the altitude indication jumped up almost a hundred feet. Now it was just over 2000.

"That's enough. Now pull up, then dive a little. That will slack the rope. Then pull the release."

Again I followed his instructions carefully. There must have still been some tension on the rope because it sprang forward like a rubber band and suddenly got full of waves. At the end of the rope we could see the steel ring flailing around. We turned left to stay clear, and the towplane turned the other way, then went into a steep dive and was out of sight. We flew alone.

Don Barnard began shouting instructions.

"Now keep an eye on your variometer. It's a German instrument marked 'Steigt' and 'Sinkt'. The higher the needle goes into the 'Steigt' the better your lift is. Right before you fly into a thermal you generally have increased sink; don't worry about it. When you get into lift you don't turn right away, but wait a few seconds. That way you don't turn out of the lift . . . . Here we are now with sink . . . . and now the lift. WOW! Look at that needle! This is a wonderful day, y'know what I mean!"

After the first moment there was no sensation of rising. We began turning left and kept on turning as the variometer needle indicated strong lift and the altimeter began to show rapid gain of altitude. In a few minutes I saw the big TG-3 again, just a little higher than us now, and we soon climbed past it. My stomach began getting queasy; in powered aircraft you do not keep flying in circles, minute after minute. We reached cloudbase 5100 feet above the ground. The turn was stopped, and we headed west-south-west for Mesa. Just short of town, we circled again and quickly got back up to the gray mist at cloudbase. The sink in between thermals was very moderate, and we cruised around the area with little work to maintain altitude.

"Boy, this is a terrific day, y'know what I mean!" Don kept shouting.

It was a brilliant morning, and the houses below, the green fields, the wide bed of the Salt River, and the Valley clear to the horizon were dappled in cloudshadow and sunlight. Even so, I wondered. After an hour, we returned to the field and the conditions were so remarkable that Don had to search for an area of heavy sink to get down without delay. By this time, my stomach was behaving so badly I thought I might be sick right in the cockpit.

The clock on the instrument panel indicated one hour and ten minutes when we landed. Don Barnard could not contain his enthusiasm about the weather. "Boy, what a day! Ten meters up everywhere! You have to look all over the sky to find a place to come down! Look at those clouds pop! There's nothing in the world like soaring, Mr. Lincoln, y'know what I mean!"

When I got out one or two people asked what I thought of my first ride. I was very polite, and they were kind enough not to notice my color which must have been pea-green at that moment.

So this was soaring? In my whole life I had never found an experience I had looked forward to for a long time so completely disappointing. From the ground, it looked effortless and graceful. There was no way of knowing the pilot might be getting sick. The sport is always compared with sailing. But in sailing there is the cry of the sea gull, the smell of salt water, and the look of a sail, full-bellied in the wind. Your boat is heeled over so the lee side is buried in water and with the pound of every swell there is new spray on your face and legs and you shiver with cold even in hot sunlight. One hand burns and the arm aches from the pull of a sheet and in the other is the steady thrust of your tiller. It is far off shore, and you cannot see the beach, only mountains which are faint and unreal through the sea-haze. And always there is the voyage you will make one day in a little schooner, sailing westward day after day, week after week, off the sea lanes, where currents make navigation difficult; in seas where it never rains—listening sometimes in terror for the shout of a lookout high on the mast: "Reef ahead," and awakening at night to look out of a port hole at a quiet sea in moonlight, the horizon dark with a row of palm trees which mark the boundary of a lagoon. . . .

In soaring, apparently all you did was fly round and round and round in circles with one eye on the variometer to see if you were going up or down and checking the altimeter once in a while to see how much, hoping in the meantime you would not get airsick. After all those years looking up at a buzzard wheeling majestically in the sky, it was a blow to discover the real thing had been so fantastically over-rated.

CHAPTER 2

Solo

The next month Don Barnard made a trip to Los Angeles where he got a Bowlus Baby Albatross, the little pod and boom sailplane which was popular in the 1930's. In pod and boom configuration there is not a complete fuselage. The pilot sits in a rather short, streamlined compartment known as a pod which contains the usual cockpit equipment and to which the wing is fixed. The tail control surfaces are attached to the outer end of a hollow boom which runs aft from the back part of this pod and the control cables for elevators and rudder are inside the boom which is often made of aluminum tubing.

After being away for over a month, one bright Sunday morning I went back to the field. I was pulled by the same magic that had made me curious about soaring for thirty years; in the bones I was unable to feel it could always be as dull and uncomfortable as it had been on my first flight. Out near the strip I saw the Baby Albatross for the first time. It was white with red trim—I thought I had never seen wings that were so graceful; the taper half way out on the leading edge was like the wrist of a gull, and the trailing edges had an exquisite curve; the pod and tail feathers looked like part of the same bird—it was small and lithe and full of youth; it trembled a little in the wind as if quivering to be airborne. I fell in love; I bought it from Don within the hour.

That Sunday the air was quite stable, "unsoarable" is the word used by pilots. I was very anxious to fly the Baby Albatross, but it is a single place aircraft, and I was not yet up to solo proficiency. I made two flights with Don Barnard in his LK, during which we did "air work," as maneuvering is called among students. The second landing went far better than previous ones, and I began to get over the feeling of impossible strangeness which at first had been so unnerving about the sailplane, with its use of full control movements.

On the way home that day, I stopped for a malted milk with Don Barnard, and we spent hours talking about soaring. He told me about some of the things which had happened in the National Contest he flew at Wichita Falls back in 1947 and some of the experiences from his long career as an instructor—about the time when he had helped launch the great Dick Johnson in his Baby Albatross; it had been a bungee or rubber rope launch from a hill and was back when Johnson was an unknown boy—even before he had gone to Elmira the first time when he was only seventeen and had astounded the older pilots. Don told the story of the BT-13 pilot who had hung around the field where he was flying. The pilot was noisy and full of disdain for what he called the little birds with no fan—one day he took off after Don who was aloft in his Baby Albatross; when the

BT-13 got almost up to the same altitude Don found a strong thermal and the BT could not stay anywhere close —even at full power and climb rate he was soon a thousand feet below. Don told of circling with buzzards and cliff soaring over Torrey Pines. The stories came without end. He was Don Barnard, the nightclub organist—but when he talked of soaring he rose to the Olympian heights of a Homeric poet.

The great excitement I had felt before my first ride began to return.

Wednesday, April fourth, the telephone rang in my stained glass studio. It was Don Barnard.

"A few of the boys are going out to the field today, can you come?"

"It's a workday," I said. "Oh well, maybe for an hour or two."

When I arrived in early afternoon, the LK, Pratt-Read, and Baby Albatross were on the line. The TG-3 was tied down on the apron, minus a wing. I asked what had happened and found that the two owners had left a wing unsecured and unattended just before a stiff gust came by. The wing had blown off the trailer and got its trailing edge caved in. The pilot who had planned to fly it was now busy in the pod of the Baby installing a variometer. He asked my permission to fly and with Don's recommendation, I said yes.

Don and I took off in the LK on a short dual ride and landed just in time to see the Baby Albatross getting airborne. Its flight was a short one. After missing two thermals the pilot got well downwind of the field and pulled spoilers for the approach. Even from our distance we could see the spoiler panels upright on the wings. They are used to steepen a glidepath without gaining speed, and the pilot now let the sailplane come down without even lowering the nose to gain speed against the wind. Somebody

DON BARNARD, *a great soaring instructor. My early flights including first solo were made in Don's LK:N53613 shown in right foreground.*

JERRY ROBERTSON *stepping out of the Pratt-Read's cockpit.*

made a nervous joke about having to pull him out of the watermelon patch, but the sailplane did not turn into the cultivated field, it did not pick up speed; it came on interminably and at last hit a wide irrigation ditch with a splintering crash that left one of the wings broken at the root and lying forward at a 45 degree angle. It was a brutal thing to see.

For a moment, all of us looked at the broken wing with desolate, helpless anger, then suddenly we realized the pilot might be hurt and ran over to have a look. There was some blood spattered about the cockpit, and we made ready to take him to the hospital, but soon found out the only damage was a minor cut on his forehead, and he told us the blow had caused a severe headache. It was an expensive lesson: if you loan your sailplane be prepared to lose it.

Three o'clock and two sailplanes broken since noon. I was sick with disgust and remembered that I was very busy, having planned to stay only an hour.

"I'll have to be going now," I said and wondered if I would ever come back.

Don Barnard must have read my thoughts.

"We have lost only three quarters of an hour," he began. "The LK is on the line, the tow ship is ready, nobody is waiting as they are on Sundays. Take just one short ride. You can be back in twenty minutes . . . ." He went on and on. Against my inclination I gave in.

The instruction ride lasted an hour and ten minutes and finally I was getting the feel of the ship. After a respectable landing, I got ready to hurry back to work. This time he stopped me with one brief sentence: "How about taking her solo?" Five instruction flights had been made; two hours and fifty-five minutes total glider time. I had no trouble this time deciding I was not too busy.

Before the solo, I needed a fifteen minute rest in order to let my stomach settle down. It was much better

FIRST SOLO, *above rough terrain in Don Barnard's LK. Four Peaks is the horizon summit. Scarface Mountain appears under sailplane.*

now, but still giving me trouble when I circled for long periods.

A cigarette, a candy bar, instructions at the last minute —safety belt and shoulder harness fastened, canopy down, altimeter set on zero, clock set at high noon; a shout and the wings held level, throbbing tense anticipation, the towline drawing taut—then the sound of the wheel rolling, the kiss of the air as I pulled off the runway, a shallow dive to let the towplane come up, and we were airborne on my first solo in a sailplane.

Just before takeoff, we had seen Derek Van Dyke fly over the field. He was now aloft in his big, side-by-side Pratt-Read sailplane, close to the field at 1800 feet. When he saw me leave the ground, he started to climb again. I released at 2000 in good lift and started after him, soaring carefully and gaining by slow degrees.

At 5400 feet, I caught him and once got 15 feet above, then lost the advantage. After working here with Derek a few minutes more, the lift weakened, and I flew north in heavy sink until getting new lift at 4000 feet over a small hill.

This time I got up to 6000, 900 feet higher than I had ever been in a sailplane and decided to try my luck over Scarface Mountain, a precipitous ridge about a thousand feet high. It was eight miles east of Falcon Field, with a broad stripe of yellow stone running horizontally across its length near the top. The mountain lies in a north-south plane, and I theorized that the strong west wind blowing against the face might produce good lift. Flying in medium sink, I used up 1200 feet of altitude getting to the north end of the ridge and turned right to fly along its crest. No lift, and I was too low to spend much time this far from the field with a headwind on the return flight.

Suddenly, I thought of turning downwind, in case lift at this altitude might be leeward of the crest. Nervously, I made the turn—a little low over very rough terrain on my first solo, with a headwind to buck on the return. I set thirty seconds as my limit. In fifteen seconds, the variometer needle jumped, then slowly went from "sinkt" to "steight;" 3 meters, 4 meters, 8 meters! 4500 feet and going up fast again. 5000, 6000, 7000, with a growing sense of triumph and achievement unlike anything I had ever experienced. Finally the altimeter showed 7600, within 650 feet of our Club altitude record. The lift weakened, and I headed home, arriving over the field with 4,000 feet to play off in a sharp spiral.

Now the landing . . . . 500 feet, just right going into the downwind leg. Remember now, just one chance! Take it easy; not too high, not too low . . . . Down to 350 feet and past the end of the strip—turn left base. Airspeed right on 50 . . . . 200 feet, now turn final; airspeed right . . . . straighten out, O. K. ease up on the speed a little—spoilers now, over the ditch with about nine feet left; now spoilers off and straight ahead, plenty of field left. Touchdown! Almost perfect!

My speed wore off and using just a little brake, I stopped a few feet from Don Barnard at the end of the runway. He bounded up to congratulate me. The grin on his face grew bigger when I told him I had made 7600 feet. Time: 1 hour and 20 minutes. I did not realize then I had forfeited membership in the informal national fraternity of power pilots and had gained admission to the world fraternity of soaring pilots. There was only one thing for me to say:

"Now I know what all the shouting is about."

CHAPTER 3

What Keeps Them Up?

Since we live in a country which thinks in terms of engine propulsion, there is widespread confusion and wonder at how a sailplane or soaring bird can stay aloft and even gain altitude without apparent effort. Old time power pilots have been known to remark, after a man has soared a hundred and fifty miles, that he must have been towed up to prodigious altitude in order to make such a flight. They thought the only way of going cross-country in a sailplane was by gliding; they were strangers to the whole concept of soaring.

Any fixed-wing aircraft has to move through the air to maintain flight. The wing of a power plane is drawn through the air by a propeller or jet engine and it can climb, fly without any change of altitude, or glide. A sailplane in flight is always descending in relation to the air, except when on tow or during a brief zoom in which speed is converted into altitude. The aircraft maintains forward motion and flying speed by descending, like a skier. The speed of his forward motion depends upon the steepness of descent, again like the skier. To get maximum velocity a man on skis will go straight down his hill. If he should be interested in maximum distance, or greater safety, he skis *across* the hill while descending. The shallower his rate of descent the farther and slower he goes, to the point where he stops or "stalls" when friction of the snow equals the downward pull of gravity. An aircraft in similar circumstances will not stop, but lose altitude suddenly in order to regain flying speed.

So far we have been gliding. Once the skier is at the bottom he is through; to get another ride he must either climb up, or be lifted up the hill so he can ski down again. It is at this point that the explanation of the difference between soaring and skiing grows complex, because skiing is like gliding in stable air. The sailpilot breaks into a sweat, orders another glass of beer and starts: "Now, if the mountainside were going up . . . ." There is difficulty carrying on like this if one does not have arms and legs for gesticulation and perhaps a washtub or other paraphernalia for demonstration.

The air, unlike the side of a mountain, can be unstable —that is, it can have vertical motion. Horizontal motion in the air is called wind; vertical motion is called instability and this instability can be caused either by heating or mechanical displacement.

In soaring, upward motion of the air is called *lift.*

Downward motion is called *sink.*

Every sailplane has a minimum sinking rate at which it must descend through the air to maintain flying speed. If the pilot flies at this rate in air which is *ascending at exactly the same speed,* he is flying in *zero sink.* The derivation of this term is easy because the sailplane maintains constant altitude above terrain even though it is sinking through the air.

If skiing compares with gliding in stable air, soaring compares to the use of ascending and descending escalators. Assuming the escalators are not moving and a man walks down, he is gliding again—forward progress goes on at a fixed rate of descent. If the escalators are working and a man gets on the "down" escalator and walks down at the same speed as before, he descends quite rapidly. This is like gliding in sink. If a man gets on the "up" escalator by mistake when it is stopped, walks half way down to the floor below, and then someone starts the escalator moving up at the same rate he is coming down, it is like soaring in zero sink. The man keeps walking down the steps, and they keep going up; but his altitude remains the same. This is tremendous fun, but an experience most people deny themselves after an early age. Even better is the sporting achievement of making it up to the floor above on the "down" escalator which gives the illusion that you have outpointed the machine and really beaten the system.

Perhaps our man has now been walking down the "up" escalator for some time at zero sink. If someone at the controls gets enthusiastic and puts extra speed into the moving stairway so our friend is actually *gaining* altitude even though still walking down, he is doing the equivalent of soaring in lift.

If the reader is now beginning to have a glimmer of comprehension about the black magic that soaring birds and sailpilots use in order to stay up without great chugging and strain and flapping of wings—but if he immediately wants to be able to impress his friends with new-found soaring erudition, he is referred to the glossary which begins on page 176. Here an attempt is made to describe all basic terms.

There is thermal soaring, ridge soaring, and wave soaring. To this list might be added shear line and frontal soaring. In all cases flight is maintained by ascending air currents which, in balance, equal or exceed the sinking rate of a glider or sailplane. Generally, cross-country soaring is done by an alternate series of climbs and glides. The flight is ended when a pilot cannot find a new thermal in which to gain altitude at the end of the day, because the sun is low and the air becoming stable, or when luck gives out on him and he flies between ascending air currents and has to go down early.

Impressive flights have been made using only atmospheric power. The world distance record is now 535 miles; the altitude record is over 46,000 feet. During a flight described later on, I spent some little time gaining height at more than 2000 feet per minute. In terms familiar to the earthbound, this is like going from the bottom of the Grand Canyon up to the level of Bright Angel Lodge in 150 seconds. (5000 feet gain of height.)

CHAPTER 4

Silver C

Even though my Baby Albatross was broken, Don Barnard assured me it could be quickly repaired, and I began looking forward to the National Soaring Contest which was going to start on the last day of July in Texas. There, I would have a chance to meet the great and see the best in American soaring. Meanwhile, our troubles at Falcon Field were not yet over. Three days after my first solo, the Pratt-Read was cracked up and broken past repair. Then Jerry Robertson, our young college high-jumping champion who had traded his little sports car for a sailplane, lost his LK fuselage in a fire at Tempe. It was a hard test for the Arizona Soaring Association. Just when things were looking up, we lost four of our ships in a period of three weeks. But Don's LK was still flying and the weather held up.

The unofficial Club altitude record was 8250 feet above terrain, set by Roy Graves in September, 1955. On April 21, 1956, Roy Smoots broke this with a flight to 8600. The following afternoon Don Barnard went to 8700. He held the record an hour and a half. On a second attempt that same day, I caught very strong lift and went to 13,100 feet, an altitude gain of 11,600. This flight lasted over two hours and was used for my C pin. It was also my first step on the long road toward the Diamond C.

The lowest of these awards, called the A Pin, is for a gliding achievement. This pin consists of a single stylized white gull set in a round field of blue. The requirements for the A Pin are two flights of forty-five seconds each, and a flight with two S turns lasting a full minute. Landings after all three flights must be normal and safe. The B Pin has two gulls in the field, one above the other. Again the requirements are of a gliding nature, but more difficult. The student must show his ability to make a 360 degree turn, both to left and right. Landings after the flights must be normal, and the towline used should not exceed five hundred feet in length, thus limiting the altitude with which the candidate must execute his maneuver. These pins date from the 1920's, during the heyday of the open, wire-laden, primary trainer gliders, and are now mainly of historical interest.

The C Pin is the lowest of the soaring pins, as opposed to gliding pins. Here the requirement is to maintain height or preferably to stay above the point of release from tow for a period of five minutes.* During the early 1930's this was a major achievement. With present day knowledge and equipment it now indicates that a pilot has advanced to solo proficiency, has made at least one soaring flight, and

---

*This is a minimum requirement for the C Pin. Subsequent to this flight, the requirements have been made more stringent by the S. S. A., which can increase requirements for the A, B and C Pins. The requirements for the more advanced soaring pins are under the international control of F. A. I.

has, in the United States, joined The Soaring Society of America. The C Badge, like the A and B, is circular. On the field of blue there are three stylized white gulls, one above another. At the top there is the letter N, which stands for United States; F is for France, G for Great Britain, etc. The more advanced Pins or Badges are called in succession, *The Silver C, Golden C, Diamond C*. At this point even the Silver C looked very advanced and remote to me.

Next week I flew a 40 mile out and return with no observer at the turn point, making it impossible to use the flight for Silver C Distance which requires a cross-country soaring flight of 50 kilometers, or 31 miles. The following week, there came a forced landing in the Salt River bed and a five-hour struggle to get the sailplane out. On June 10, I received my private glider license. July first, the Baby Albatross finally got out of the hospital, and I was air towed back to Falcon. July was filled with efforts at Silver C Duration: five hours of free flight. They were all failures and many flights were not over half an hour long. Time before the National Soaring Contest was getting very short and the rules published in SOARING said you had to have a Silver C to qualify. Then new rules came out from the Texas Soaring Association requiring only Silver C Distance. I had neither.

On July 22nd, I had the good fortune to line up a crew for the National Contest. They were two boys from Tucson, Arizona, and arrangements were made to pick them up at their homes the next Sunday. We left Tucson at three o'clock Sunday afternoon and got to Grand Prairie, Texas, between Fort Worth and Dallas, twenty-eight hours later after having driven well over a 1000 miles. We arrived at Contest Headquarters during a pilots' meeting.

That first night remains a little confused. There was the pilots' meeting and registration, and the happy discov-

A Emblem

B Emblem

C Emblem

Silver or Golden C

Diamond C

Soaring Emblems

ery that I could compete the first day even without the Silver Distance requirement. There was a rush to the Lennox Hotel to get a room, then back to the field where we parked the Bowlus and saw the great RJ-5 sailplane for the first time. Her new owner, the handsome and gentle English pilot, Graham Thomson, was bent over in its cockpit, swearing like a naval officer as he tried to finish a last detail in the rigging. We met Wally Wiberg, one of the contest directors, and had Dick Johnson pointed out—the man who had won four National Soaring Contests in the RJ-5 and had flown it to the world distance record of 535 miles. I got the name Reeves attached to the "E. J." whom I had previously known only as a writer in SOARING. By midnight, we had unpacked and collapsed in bed.

FIRST CONTEST DAY

After the pilots' meeting at 8:00 A. M. we rigged the Baby Albatross, finishing just in time for opening ceremonies. There were speeches and pictures, then the Nelson Hummingbird went aloft with a General for the first flight of the contest. The Hummingbird is a big sailplane with two seats and a retractable engine for launching and retrieving itself. I began to connect faces to the names I had seen in The Soaring Society of America's Directory, champions and record holders. After seeing the *Jenny Mae* go off on her first flight, I got set for my own initial tow.

I was one of the last pilots off, behind a towplane acting like it was determined to crack the sound barrier. After the crash in April, the Baby had been repaired as an open cockpit ship, and I was realizing a life-long ambition to fly in the open. Sixty-five miles an hour is redline speed for the Baby Albatross; to go any faster endangers the structure in case of gusts or sudden control stick forces. We were now flying 85 miles per hour, and I was hearing some amazing sounds. The control wheel was held nearly

28

still to keep from loading the wings any more than necessary, but I kept thinking of what Don Barnard had said: "It's a fine little aircraft if you don't push it past its limitations. Very lightly built you know." He also mentioned that one had come apart in the 1947 National Soaring Contest. Maybe I should have gone fishing this summer instead? At 1800 feet the towplane went into a steep dive. I took the hint that he wanted to go home and released the line which was taut as a violin string.

The task set by the contest committee was to fly to Mineral Wells and back. It was during the strongest part of the day, and I soared rapidly up to 7000 feet before striking west.

Arlington went by slowly underneath, with its rows of neat little houses and green yards; then the newly completed earthen dam to the west which would one day be a reservoir, and the tall buildings of downtown Fort Worth, and Carswell Air Force Base, which had been called Tarrant Field and had been a training base for B-24 pilots when I had served there during the war thirteen years ago. After a long time, the lake north of Mineral Wells came into sight. That morning, it was hot on the ground, and I had left my jacket with the crew. It was amazingly cold now at 8000 feet. At last came the upwind beat into Mineral Wells, identification of markers and the turn. We were getting low; conditions were weak in the late afternoon and no amount of work seemed to gain back altitude. After a short retreat, we landed at the turn point.

The task of a crew is to follow their pilot with a car and trailer, find him, de-rig, and retrieve the sailplane while the pilot sleeps peacefully in the back of the car, dreaming about his flight coming up tomorrow. In modern contest soaring, two-way, battery-operated radios make this job much easier than it used to be. Flights are often made with pilot and crew in radio communication all the way. I had no radio equipment, so we had to learn the old-fashioned method of crewing, in which a crew acts on its knowledge of the approximate wind conditions, thermal strength, pilot ability and performance of his aircraft. They also know the direction the flight will probably take to be in accordance with the task the contest committee sets for the day. Using this information, a skillful crew can find a downed sailplane in amazingly short time if luck is good. When the day wears on and a crew thinks their pilot is likely to be down, they make telephone calls to contest headquarters with increasing frequency. As soon as the pilot lands and secures his aircraft, he calls headquarters giving his position, generally in coordinates of latitude and longitude from his air chart, along with other descriptive information which could help his crew. My own youthful crew was magnificent this first time; they arrived in five minutes.

Silver C Distance! Mineral Wells was almost a hundred kilometers from Grand Prairie and the requirement was only fifty. Tall, slender Connie Ripley was at the turnpoint that day. She always had a joke and a word of help, and spent half her time crewing and half of it helping the contest directors. To get contest points, a pilot carries landing cards which must be signed by at least two landing witnesses, to verify the flight distance made good. Pilots also carry application forms which must be filled out if any flight is good for a Silver, Golden, or Diamond C leg. In any flight involving distance, two landing witnesses must sign these applications which are filled out, specifying the pilot's name, date, sailplane, takeoff point, distance flown, altitude of take off and landing points, etc. The forms are then sent to The Soaring Society of America for investigation and processing. I got Connie to sign my landing cards and the application for my Silver C Distance leg. I also got the airport manager, the airline people, and the girl behind the food counter to sign. This thing had to be sure! We all returned to Grand Prairie in triumph, then Wally Wiberg reduced my head of steam:

"You've got to have a barograph trace to make your Silver C Distance flight official," he said. "Would you like to use this barograph tomorrow?"

Another defeat. I had flown the necessary distance, but it would not count. The rule stated that a pilot must either have a barogram (barograph trace) or be continuously observed throughout his flight by an official observer of The Soaring Society.

A soaring barograph is a recording barometer, calibrated in altitude, which can be sealed and opened by an official observer of The Society and which produces a trace or record of altitude throughout a flight. One of these traces, properly authenticated, can be used as proof of continuous flight from takeoff to landing on a record attempt or a flight for one of the Soaring Badges. Wally Wiberg now handed me a Peravia, an elegant Swiss barograph which makes a trace on waxed paper. This is easier to handle and more readable than the kind I had been using. It belonged to the contest director, E. J. Reeves, and was the first one I had ever seen. Carefully guarding the precious instrument, we returned to the hotel.

SECOND DAY

Today was open and a downwind run was indicated. The Baby Albatross and I got off much earlier, but had a slow start during which all the other sailplanes were being very careful and holding on to every foot of altitude. After an hour, things picked up, and we got north of Denton before getting into any kind of trouble. Then altitude ran out, and we were down to 1400 feet before getting new lift.

After some very anxious work things got better and we flew on, getting under a cloudstreet just south of the Red River. A cloudstreet is a series of cumulus clouds lined up in a row, under which a sailplane can fly straight, without circling to gain or maintain altitude. This was my first time under a street and the feel of roaring along at a steady 45 miles an hour without circling gave me a tremendous thrill. The time of reckoning came when the cloudstreet got wet. I began to circle in weak lift which turned into zero sink, then to rapidly increasing sink. We left the clouds at 4500 and struck off on course at maximum glide in dead calm air. At 500 feet there were two little bumps over Wirt, Oklahoma, but not enough to keep us going, so we turned back and landed half a mile south of town. The call to contest headquarters was difficult to get through. We had flown 108 miles in three and a half hours and this time had a barograph trace in hand. My Silver C Leg had at last been won.

THIRD DAY

One hundred and eight miles had seemed good until I found out Maxey and Schreder had gone clear to Wichita, having outfoxed the dead area that brought me down. Feeling blue and incompetent, I prepared for the day's flight, a 300 kilometer triangle to Mineral Wells, Lake Whitney and back. An alto-stratus layer had come in from the south and a good number of sailplanes landed after their first tow. The Bowlus followed them down. Feeling even worse, I got ready for another try.

The day was weak by Texas standards. I worked my way to the near side of Fort Worth and gave up, turned around and headed back for Grand Prairie. Suddenly came the realization that I was not even going to get back, and a difficult landing was made five miles west of Arlington.

The best contest flight of any day earns a pilot 1000

CONTEST SOARING. *Jock Forbes, one time English Soaring Champion, takes off at a U. S. National Soaring Contest.*

FIRST CONTEST FLIGHT. *Going aloft in my Baby Albatross during the Twenty-third National Soaring Contest.*

points. Using a combination of speed and distance fac-
tors, the scoring committee works out scores for all contestants. Five hundred points indicates a flight which is
half as good as the best flight of the day. A pilot who gets
less than 800 points on any single day has a rather poor
chance of winning. That day I made 59.

FOURTH DAY

The task was an out and return flight to Mineral Wells.
My takeoff time was quite early and the first part of the
flight was like a ride on a pogo stick. Release and climb to
3900, then down to 1800, up to 3300, down to 1500, all
within a few miles of the field. One hour out, I was tearing
past Arlington only six miles away at 5000 feet; two hours
put me over Carswell Air Force Base. Forty minutes later,
soon after working a very rough thermal west of Lake
Worth, I was in trouble again. Lift had run out, and I was
down below 1400. This was a miserable thing during the
strongest part of the day. I looked over the fields and
watched the variometer intently.

Then came lift, and very strong! In fifteen minutes
we were at 8000 feet and going faster than at any time
since takeoff. Weatherford slowly came into sight, then
the Army Camp, and Mineral Wells with its familiar airport where I had landed the first day and which was again
the turn point. Time was building up: 4:10, 4:23, 4:40.
Silver C Duration?

The altitude and distance tests for the Silver C must
be accomplished on separate flights; duration may be com-
bined with either one. Two days before, I had made the
Distance with the flight of 108 miles; the requirement is
only 31.1, 50 kilometers. The Silver C altitude gain was
now recorded on my barograph with plenty to spare. The
requirement is a gain of 1000 meters, 3281 feet above the
low point after release; I had gained over 6000 feet that

afternoon. But the Duration—five long hours after release from tow!

I thought of Terence Horsley who had described his long flight in the open cockpit sailplane, how the rain had beaten his face and finally put so much water in the fuselage he had to land. Three hours and forty-five minutes. I was now almost an hour ahead of him, but it was getting late. I thought of the Silver C Pin—three white gulls on their blue field surrounded by a laurel wreath of silver. The names of Silver C pilots were internationally recorded. Could I go home with that honor?

Half a mile south of the field at Mineral Wells, I made a decision to hang onto any lift that came since I had used up 3000 feet running south into the wind to identify the marker. At 4200 feet lift came, and we drifted northward, slowly gaining altitude. At 6600 I could get no higher, but it was now five hours since I had left the ground. Eight more minutes for the tow, and I would have it. We came down very slowly, flying at minimum sink in a very weak thermal which did not have quite enough lift to keep us airborne.

At 5:10 after takeoff, I picked a good field and ran a long series of figure eights downwind of the approach. The touchdown was at 5:15. After such a long flight the ticking of the barograph sounded very loud. When I turned it off, I sat in the cockpit for a long minute with a feeling of absolute elation which can only be understood by those with logbooks which record many failures in trying for this leg of the Silver C. I had graduated!

FIFTH DAY

Saturday, the second open day. I made an excellent start and was passing over Grapevine Reservoir twenty-five miles out with over 6000 feet in hand. Prospects looked very good for making Golden C Distance, but gradually my altitude slipped away without lift and at 3000 I knew I had a long climb ahead; at 2000 I grew alarmed. Finally at 1200 the lift came; two turns at zero sink with a couple of puffs, then the bottom fell out even though I had selected an area in wind shadow. Eight hundred feet, then 600, and I knew a landing was ahead.

The field was lovely. It was a grassy meadow with shade trees between well-kept farms, but I landed in misery. One o'clock, the height of the day, and I was down. I told myself that I was a beginner with no experience; you can't expect to win the Indianapolis race in a Model-T Ford, you just came for the laughs. It was no good. I felt like crawling into a hole and staying there .Three hundred and twenty miles was par for the course that day; fourteen flights carried over three hundred. I made thirty-six.

SIXTH DAY

The 300 kilometer triangle again: Mineral Wells, Lake Whitney and home. I released from tow at 1300 and soared to cloudbase with unusual speed. My takeoff timing was an amazing bit of luck because the sky was gray and unpromising, still it gave me the strongest lift of the meet and I was under a cloudstreet from the time I reached base. The weather at 8000 under cloudshadow was freezing in an open cockpit sailplane. Ten miles out I had the Baby on redline and was still gaining altitude at 800 feet a minute. Having no turn-and-bank, no compass no instrument experience and no Texas cloudmap, I discreetly slid out to the edge of the lift and went on. Beyond Fort Worth, I made a first stop to circle for altitude, less than a dozen turns, and I was at Weatherford before having to do any real work. Back at 7000 I headed for Mineral Wells, and over the turn point I got my biggest thermal of the contest. It carried up to 10,000 where the air was so cold I was afraid of freezing solid. I tightened the belly and pulled my jacket on backwards as far as it would go. Then began a long glide against the strong head wind. Halfway down I circled for a while with Bill Coverdale in his dark blue Skylark and then pressed on. Lift grew weaker and weaker because of the overcast and finally I was standing still; each climb and glide put me over the same point. I headed on course for the day's last glide and made my best score of the meet.

When the crew arrived, and we had my sailplane back on its trailer, we started toward the main road, then turned on a little country byway which took us over an ancient, rickety, wooden bridge across the Brazos River. We parked and went down for a long swim. The gray afternoon was balmy, the river warm; there was a soaring flight behind and another one coming tomorrow. It was an afternoon too full of peace to describe, with a lovely western river quietly flowing between tree-lined banks, under a wooden bridge that might have been the work of a pioneer.

SEVENTH DAY

The task was an out and return to Breckenridge, Texas, 108 miles away. I got in trouble shortly after leaving tow. On downwind leg for a return to the field, I hit a weak thermal at 600 feet. I'll show these people who can fly, I thought to myself. Up we went to 800 and 1000 feet where I noticed we had drifted beyond gliding range to the field —but what does it matter? Still going up. Then suddenly, I was hanging in the balance between gravity and thermal pull. Several turns followed with rising desperation, but it was too late. A few minutes later I landed in a corn field under a sky of beautiful cumulus clouds in all directions as far as the eye could see. I got out and spat. Even the gods had to rub it in that day: seconds after touchdown, a thermal came by which was so strong it tempted me to try getting aloft without even using a tow.

I went up to a farm house and called my crew. They had just left the field. The farmer and I talked, then I called again, then talked some more and called again. Several hours later they arrived, having gone the wrong way, and having gone for a swim where they met some girls.

We were the first home, beating even *Jenny Mae,* the beautiful red and white sailplane flown by silent Lyle Maxey, the team which had been in first place since opening day. There was a small difference though. We had to drive home and missed the turnpoint by a small margin of 104 miles.

LAST DAY

A triangle flight to Russell Field, Denton, and back. Scores had to be in by four o'clock because the awards banquet was that night.

After a good start, I fell into a hole short of Russell Field, worked my way up a little, then fell clear down and had to land there. Interestingly, it was the same hole that gave Maxey his last scare of the contest. A few minutes after I was down, he passed over us at 6000 feet and the *Jenny Mae* flew north, regal and triumphant. At her next landing, she brought home the champion of the United States.

I called my crew and waited, called and waited, read a magazine, called and waited. They had gone hunting for something else that day. After four hours, I called for a tow home, and Gus Briegleb came in with the TSA Waco. I released at Arlington and glided back through silken air.

At the awards banquet in Fort Worth that night, Tony Page gave me her Tail End Tony Trophy for having proven beyond any reasonable doubt that I was the worst soaring pilot in the United States; and then, in the absence of anyone else being in my bracket, I was given the Plaque for National Class C Champion, presented by Dick Johnson himself.

I made two more attempts at the 300 kilometer Golden Distance flight before leaving Texas. One of them carried 130 miles without a tailwind.

At last it was time to leave. I had lunch in Dallas that day with E. J. Reeves, and we talked about soaring. Then I went back to the Lennox Hotel in Grand Prairie and packed. I took a last look at my room where I had kept the precious barograms which were now already sent off to Ben Shupack with my application for a Silver C Pin. June and Wally Wiberg had taken my Baby Albatross out to their Flying W Ranch after the last flight, and with evening drawing on I went out to pick it up and say goodbye; a goodbye full of sorrow that I was having to leave Texas and the soaring world I had just discovered.

In the early darkness, I headed west—through Grand Prairie, Arlington, Fort Worth, Weatherford, and Mineral Wells—all places I had soared over. In the mirror I could see the wingroots of my Baby Albatross, gleaming red from the tail lights; and the pod which was outlined as a shadow from the lights of cars behind. In the back seat were my Tail End Tony Trophy, the Plaque, and a Texas Soaring Association banner which had been made to celebrate the 23rd National Soaring Contest.

I also carried home the memories of that first evening in Grand Prairie when I had met E. J. Reeves and Wally Wiberg and Connie Ripley; the thrill of fear on the opening contest day when the towplane had us going far past redline; and the feel and sound of rushing air under wings in the strong burst of energy which is a thermal that sends your variometer needle to the top; and seeing leaves of corn fifteen hundred feet above the earth, falling slowly after being carried so high by a powerful updraft. There

Soaring

was the anxiety of that long afternoon when the hands of my watch had crept, with infinite deliberation, toward the five-hour mark, then passed it, and I knew I had won the Silver C. And the look of a cloudstreet getting overburdened and wet as a pilot soars over the Red River; and circling with Bill Coverdale who was in his blue Skylark, and being exalted by the sight of the RJ-5 turning in the air. I was taking home a memory of the *Jenny Mae* getting airborne on tow—its drooping slender wings rising to straightness as the speed increased, then bending upward as the sailplane left the ground, as if in gesture of thankful prayer for the glory of flight; and the memory of her pilot, Lyle Maxey, receiving the trophy of National Championship. I remembered the rickety bridge across the Brazos River on that warm, overcast afternoon; and the voice of Dick Johnson, and silent John Nowak and all the others—the soaring people, like no other people on earth because their love of the sky is so great. And I took home the laughing-light feel in the chest that comes when you are soaring under a strong cloud and there are fairweather cumuli in all directions to the horizon and you hope it will not ever end.

I never really came down from those flights.

CHAPTER 5

Back To Arizona

When I returned to Scottsdale, the real drama of the season was over. In September of 1956, the first newsletter of the Arizona Soaring Association, ARIZONA AIR CUR-RENTS, was published. Don Barnard was the only other member of our club who had competed in a National Contest, and I found myself a local celebrity in soaring. I was elected to the presidency of the Association and late that autumn, after giving it much thought, I decided to buy a Schweizer 1-23D. Weekends, I went to the field and cornered anyone who could give me any information about new parachutes, oxygen gear, instruments, radios or barographs.

The next out-of-town event was the mid-winter soaring contest at Torrey Pines. I had missed it the year before, when the Arizona group had done so well, since it

Soaring

came the week after my first ride with Don. Everybody in soaring knows about the contest at Torrey Pines, just north of La Jolla, California. Actually, there are two annual midwinter contests: the one I go to and the one which is not rained out. A number of us went including Don Barnard, and Chuck and Sally Schmid with their five-year old daughter, Cheryl. The afternoon before the contest was to begin, I had my first two winch flights in which a sailplane is towed aloft by a winch that draws up tow cable onto a drum at 50 to 70 miles per hour, much like a fish being brought in by a gigantic power reel. Both flights lasted one minute. Next day, the contest was rained out, but I had a longer flight in late afternoon along the cliffs. It lasted three minutes before I landed on the beach. This was a long comedown from my dream of setting a new duration record over the cliffs in my Baby Albatross.

There were long, pleasant intervals of hangar flying and talking to pilots I had met the summer before at Grand Prairie. I returned home by way of Los Angeles because I wanted to meet Lynn Brown and talk about Skycrafter radios for my new sailplane, and wanted to see Zep Aero about high altitude oxygen equipment. When the trip was over, I had made a record of sorts: I trailed the Baby Albatross more than 1300 miles for a total of five minutes flying.

One conversation of that weekend stays in mind. It was between Captain Schmid and his little daughter, Cheryl. After listening for hours to soaring talk, she decided it was pretentious.

"You can't fly as good as the birds, Daddy," she said.
"Oh yes, I can fly better than the birds."
"You can't fly as high as the birds."
"Yes. I can fly even higher than the birds."
"You can't fly as fast as the birds."
"Oh, I can fly much faster than any bird."

42

TOWLINE CONNECTION. *Ken Bawden is connecting the steel ring of the towline to the TG-3's towhook. Bob Wister in the cockpit.*

THE WINCH *is going at full power and drawing in cable at 50-70 mph.*

The child gave him a long, hard and furious look.
"Well, you can't build a nest."

Bob Hawkes purchased my Baby Albatross in the spring and through the winter months that year, I planned a Diamond Goal flight to Douglas in the Pratt-Read sailplane, a big two-place aircraft which a group of us had bought the previous autumn.

Sunday, March 3, 1957, was a day of beautiful cumulus clouds. I had intended to drive my children out to Cave Creek that afternoon, but the sky looked too full of soaring promise to miss. I called Sally Schmid and found that Chuck had no crew. He lacked only the distance leg to make his Silver C. I raced out to Falcon Field to offer my service as a crewman and at 3:20 he was airborne in the Pratt-Read with a sealed barograph running to record his flight.

Fifteen minutes after takeoff, Captain Schmid turned east on course with what appeared to be good altitude. His goal was Superior Airport, 38 miles away, Silver C Distance. We left immediately with my Ford and Pratt-Read trailer and maintained a speed over 60 miles an hour almost all the way to Apache Junction before catching up with him the first time. After five minutes there, we started off again on the way to Florence Junction. His speed was excellent. There was a small break in cloud development east of Apache Junction, but he made contact with good clouds. I thought the next stop might be Superior, and we would have a new Silver C pilot in our ranks. He seemed only a little short of straight gliding distance away, since there was a strong tail wind.

Half way to Florence Junction, we passed him again after he had stopped to circle. This time it was a much longer stop. After fifteen minutes, we drove two miles into the "Don's Trek" road toward Superstition Mountain. His altitude was still good, but Chuck was having trouble. I

SOARING OVER TORREY PINES. *Two sailplanes fly above the cliffs.*

thought momentarily of flagging traffic on this almost unused road to give him a chance to get down if necessary. The good clouds were moving eastward rapidly while he was holding position above a steep little ridge which evidently produced intermittent lift. Lower and lower came the sailplane, below the crest of the mountain, then just above it, then down again, always getting lower as each thermal gave out. We turned around, got out to the main highway, and lost sight of him. At the entrance to the King Ranch, there was a boy waiting. I turned the car in, picked him up, and got the news: Chuck had gone down behind the ridge. Where? The country was rough and had a heavy growth of saguaros, cholla, ironwood, greasewood, and palo-verde. We headed in.

Just past the ridge, the country got much worse. Every hundred yards we travelled, I got less worried about the sailplane and more worried about Chuck Schmid. A fork in the road. Which way? We tried right. In half a mile we came to a house where we found Ken Bawden and Willy Rogers, both members of the Arizona Soaring Association who had followed in their own car to watch the Pratt-Reed's flight. The owner of the house had seen Chuck go down, and he offered to lead us to the place, and Chuck walked out to meet us, looking very embarrassed.

"Are you OK?" I asked anxiously.

"No sweat." So far so good.

"How is the aircraft? The man said you just banged up a wingtip."

"It's bad enough."

We left the car—one crewman, four children, two dogs, Willie, Kenny, and Chuck. A hundred yards off the road, we came to the sailplane, which was headed into the wind with stones over a cushion on the wing that was down. Its right arm was broken at the inboard end of the aileron and was hanging down forlornly, swinging in the wind. Marcel Godinat, our Swiss Golden C pilot, was undoing the control cables. It took an hour and a half to de-rig the ship and load it on the trailer for our trip back. No Silver C today.

Half an hour before, during the landing, he had come in low and had to make a last minute decision not to use the road because it was fenced and lined with palo-verde trees which had not shown up from the air; he came around a low bluff, past a house, over the wires, and down into a clear space not much bigger than a basketball court—all in a gusty crosswind. Fifty feet to either side, 10 feet too high or low, and the sailplane would have been kindling, and Chuck Schmid might have been hurt badly. That landing was made with high self-confidence and extra-ordinary skill. With a little more luck, he would have only scratched paint. Bad fortune came when he struck an ironwood tree, slender as the arm of a child, but strong as steel. It broke the wing. Anyone subject to getting rattled after such an agonizing letdown would have been in serious danger.

The crackup ended my chance of making a Diamond Goal flight that spring. I had dreamed of being the first man to soar from Mesa to Douglas, Arizona, which was over 300 kilometers away so it would be Golden C Distance, and landing at the little airport east of town—my Goal—my first Diamond. Now there could be no cross-county soaring until my 1-23D was finished back in El-mira; little chance of spreading my wings before the National Soaring Contest in July.

CHAPTER 6

Cirro-Q

After almost eleven months of waiting since the end of the contest at Grand Prairie, in late June, 1957, came the time to leave for the 24th National Soaring Contest at Elmira, New York. The trip east with my crewchief Jerry Robertson was full of anticipation. We were heading for my first National to be flown with a first-class sailplane and a good crew.

After packing for the trip and taking care of last minute business chores, we left my Studio in Scottsdale at one thirty in the morning. At breakfast time we were up north of Globe and ate at a place in the bottom of the Salt River Canyon. By early afternoon, we were in Gallup, New Mexico. Then we drove eastward through a golden day, past Albuquerque, Clines Corners, and Santa Rosa, and the whole world was touched with the magic things

48

have when a person is newly in love. When we stopped for supper in Tucumcari, it was growing dark.

That night, I drove northeastward while Jerry slept in the back. On the horizon ahead, beyond Dalhart, there grew the most enormous and beautiful cumulonimbus cloud I have ever seen in the dark, towering about 40,000 feet in the air. Lightning kept flashing inside the cloud, and I watched it grow and change in the momentary flashes of illumination. We caught up with the storm in the Oklahoma Panhandle and for a time the rain was so heavy I had to cut driving speed down to five miles an hour. There was flooding in Kansas, and we drove a hundred miles out of our way, bypassing areas which were inundated.

That afternoon, we stopped in Wichita and as evening came, we were passing along the Missouri River beyond Kansas City. We kept pressing eastward, covering almost a thousand miles a day. In the ghostly light of dawn, we came into Elmira and immediately went to the Schweizer Factory. It was dark and the gate was locked, but inside the fence we could faintly see a 1-23D tied down, back of the factory near the little stand of pines that separates the Schweizer Building from Chemung County Airport. It was a moment I had waited for since winter.

I had seen my new sailplane only once before, that spring, a day or two after it was finished, even before it was painted, when it still wore the chartreuse color of zinc chromate. My intention had been to name it *Cirrus*, after the high, lovely ice-crystal clouds, but I found out this name had been used several times before. The cumulus cloud is the one of most importance to the soaring pilot because it indicates the generation of lift. In the cold, remote cirrus region of the lower stratosphere, when cirrus coagulates and becomes puffy, it is named cirrocumulus, or cirro-cu. I modified this to *Cirro-Q for the* name of my sailplane. After a long, thrilled look through the fence while the dark sky became gray, we left, got a motel room and slept until early afternoon.

There was much final installation and checking work to be done on the ship, and I did not fly it until the next day. All the plans and preparations made since leaving Texas the year before were now coming together. Before my first year in soaring was over, I had decided to buy a Schweizer 1-23D, rugged, stable and beautiful. I acquired a new parachute from Mr. McElfish in Dallas, Texas. There had been a voluminous correspondence with Paul Schweizer and Ron Wilcox at Schweizer Aircraft. I had to learn everything almost from the beginning and needed advice on sailplane radios, oxygen equipment, instruments, trailers. Decisions had to be made on equipment and even paint color.

My instrument panel was completed and the instrumentation was excellent. It had been worked out mainly on the advice of Wally Wiberg. During the winter, I had spent several evenings with him at the Flying W Ranch in Cedar Hill, southwest of Dallas, Texas, learning about instruments and trying to position them intelligently on the panel—help that was gratefully received because until recently I had been a power pilot and knew nothing of soaring instrumentation. My oxygen equipment was a Zep Aero pressure breathing system which was good up to 40,000 feet, 43,000 in brief emergency. I had new Skycrafter radios for both sailplane and crew car.

That first day in Elmira, I had the name *Cirro-Q* painted on each side of the handsome gray and red sailplane. I had to learn to rig and de-rig it; the ship was new and consequently stiff. A bracket had to be put in to hold the barographs. There were tools to buy which were peculiar to the fittings on this aircraft, and I needed to get a new cushion to sit on.

RIGGING BEGINS *with putting on a wing. Ruth Petry is holding the tip; Joe Vest holds the trailing edge and fuselage.*

STARTING A RETRIEVE. *Cirro-Q is de-rigged and ready to go back on its trailer after landing in a plowed field.*

Soaring

Early in the afternoon of the second day, after the essentials of this program had been taken care of, *Cirro-Q* was rigged and parked on the flight line of Chemung County Airport, and I waited for my first tow. Bernie Carris, chief flight instructor at Schweizer Aircraft, gave me last instructions on how to fly it and recommended speeds for thermalling, approach and landing. Then the canopy came down, Jerry Robertson ran the wingtip, and I went off on the first flight, rising over the beautiful Chemung Valley, and being towed past famous Harris Hill. It was the 26th of June.

The sailplane was magnificent. It was more fun to fly than any aircraft I had ever been in, with or without power. When I was aloft, I got a feeling of exaltation just looking out along the leading edge of that slender, powerful wing. I never had any special skill at spot landings and was very impressed when, on the third day of practice, I consistently put *Cirro-Q* down beyond a line and could stop within less than two hundred feet. This gave a wonderful confidence in short field ability which is necessary to competition flying.

The final installation work on the ship was very time consuming and because of it my practice flying before the contest was limited to four days. I had been flying every other day, practicing thermal soaring and landings; then on Sunday, June 30th, two days before the Contest was to begin, conditions looked very promising for an extended cross-country flight. Weather was checked and there were excellent cumulus clouds over a large area with a wind of 25 knots from west-northwest. I set a goal at Waterbury, Connecticut, 202 miles downwind, saddled up and was towed aloft from Chemung County Airport a few minutes before noon, having been hurried off by Bob Brown, who was anxious to go in his *Zanonia*. Everything was done but the ground radio check. I could not reach

Jerry in the crew car and made the flight in radio silence.

After circling only five minutes, I knew conditions were as good as they looked, and I let the sailplane drift with the wind while getting up to cloudbase. Half an hour out, I was accidentally pulled into cloud. The 1-23D is extremely sensitive on the rudder in instrument flight, and the needle of the turn-and-bank pegs at the slightest excuse. A thousand feet up in the cloud everything went wrong. Speed picked up in what I supposed was the beginning of a spiral dive, and I was frightened enough that I tried to spin out. There was a violent flip, then all speed vanished and for a moment there was complete, unearthly lack of sound. I got sick and began to try more needle-ball-and-airspeed flying in which, to get out of cloud, you try to keep the needle of the turn-and-bank instrument centered, indicating you are flying in a straight line; try to keep the ball of the ball bank centered, indicating you are reasonably level, and try to keep your airspeed somewhere around fifty miles per hour, which is over ten miles per hour faster than stall speed in the 1-23D, but slow enough that no gust could have any damaging effect.

In one or two minutes, we came out the side of the cloud, I felt as if I had emerged from a washing machine. After that, I was careful to get no higher than cloudbase, and after one hour, we were 44 miles out, nearing Binghamton. We were almost let down 60 miles along the course, and I was so miserable and airsick I almost wished for a landing, but was too stubborn to quit. In two hours, *Cirro-Q* and I were 96 miles out, right on course. I thought that four hours would give me Golden Distance with a Diamond for the Goal.

Then rain began to press me from behind, and to the north. Ahead the clouds vanished, all in a fifteen minute period. I found myself over a wooded area with one possible landing place after the lift had stopped. Slowly altitude was paid out in a search for new lift, but there was neither lift or sink, and we settled toward the earth at the gradual sinking speed of my sailplane. It was like being an animal tied to a post by a long rope, walking round and round. The lower I got, the closer I had to stay to my one field. Time: 2:25 after takeoff, 127 miles out, less than my best in the Bowlus. Lady Luck had taken the Sunday off, and I knew I was in for a landing by the time I was 800 feet above ground, so a pattern was set up, and two S turns were made to get rid of excess altitude. No lift or sink had been encountered for the last ten minutes; then, on a final approach, we hit a downdraft of 900 feet a minute! Approach speed in the 1-23D is 50 miles per hour in non-turbulent conditions. The only possible thing to do now was dive for speed, more *speed*.

Without an instant's hesitation, the nose was dropped and speed went up to 63, but we got down fifteen feet below the trees in front, and my mind's eye saw a broken sailplane hanging in the timber, smashed on its first cross-country. Only ten feet above ground the sinker could no longer exist, and we executed a roller coaster maneuver —up over the trees with the extra speed, then down over the border of my field, up onto the inclined slope—spoilers, touchdown. A hundred foot roll and we stopped. Silence. Only the ticking of my Peravia barograph as I sat exhausted in the cockpit. Then it began to rain gently. In a few minutes two New Yorkers, panting uncontrollably, came up to remove the body. They had been running up hill for half a mile, having seen me crash beyond the trees.

"Been in this country for years on summer vacations; we didn't know there was a field back here."

They were wonderfully helpful in getting the ship secured and making contact with Jerry Robertson and when all this was done, they took me home and served a Sunday dinner with wine. My stomach was in rebellion still, and wine has never been consumed with such reluctance.

After three hours, Jerry got there and the people helped us get the car and trailer up the narrow muddy road to the field where *Cirro-Q* was down. Then we made our way across the wet, slippery grass. They helped us de-rig the sailplane and when we left for Harris Hill in late afternoon, it was like saying goodbye to old friends.

The terrain is extraordinarily beautiful in this part of New York, with streams tightly contained in their narrow valleys, an occasional stately river, quiet little towns and ridge after ridge clothed in verdant green which the eye accustomed to desert country never tires of seeing. At that northern latitude, sunset is late and twilight is long, but it was almost dark when we stopped for supper. On the road again, we were amazed to see light still on the western horizon—growing stronger. Presently, I realized it was the Aurora, which in time spread over two thirds of the sky in a majestic spectacle. A good omen I thought; perhaps Nature is prepared to outdo herself for this contest.

CHAPTER 7

A National Soaring Contest at Elmira

On Harris Hill, things were dark and quiet. A freezing wind blew out of the north, brought in by an intense cold front which had just passed over. One o'clock in the morning. July was here; the sailplanes had arrived and were secured; the pilots were asleep. The battle would start tomorrow.

There were thirty-one pilots competing and thirty-one pilots out for blood. Florida sent up the veteran Fritz Compton with his ancient LK, and also the newcomer John Randall. Maxey was flying a little butterfly-tail Prue 215-A, Bikle, the 1-23E. The Londoners, Graham and Helen Thomson, had brought their newly-painted RJ-5 to the meet. The RJ-5 is a masterpiece built by Harland Ross. In addition to its great competitive record with Dick Johnson flying, last year Graham had flown it into second place in Texas, the first year he owned it. His hopes were high. Ray Parker was going to fly his golden little Tiny Mite, and Dick Schreder was there with his magnificent HP-7. It is generally considered a job of five years to build a very high performance sailplane, even if one should have the rare combination of talent and training necessary to undertake it. Dick Schreder and his friends built the HP-7 in five months. The United States is the only soaring country where homebuilt sailplanes are a major part of a national soaring movement. A picture of the HP-7 had appeared on the most recent cover of SOARING magazine, along with the story of its construction, and when it first appeared on Harris Hill, people thronged around to have a close look. It was like an inspired work of art, without a single detail one could find to regret—It was slender, white and virginal, with speed and grace built into every line.

Four Diamonds, the National Champion, and three of the first four places in the Texas 23rd National, each thinking maybe this contest was his.

The air was full of talk about the chances for a dark horse victory. "This one is going to the man who can fly on weak days," ran the story. A dozen pilots might have been dark horses, of whom the outstanding example was George Coder from Arlington, Texas. Coder brought his elegant, newly refinished Weihe, with narrow, white wings that had a span of almost sixty feet. It was a lovely bird; the highest performance sailplane the Germans had made just before the war. I even flattered myself that I might be a dark horse and it was only after two days of flying that I had to face up to being a draft horse instead. I have an excuse. My best friends did not tell me about the polar weather. I suggest the following minimum list of essential equipment for an Elmira contest:

1 Eskimo suit
1 Twenty-gallon hot water heater
1 Bedwarming pan, charcoal type
1 Dozen heavy blankets
1 Portable heater to defrost wings and toes.
   Assorted gloves, electrically heated socks, etc.
1 Sailplane

At pilots' meeting the first day, Barney Wiggin stood up to fill us in on the weather. Slender, handsome, distinguished of face and speech, he began his esoteric briefing. The picture was a little complicated. A polar blizzard had become tangled up with the back end of a southern hurricane, leaving a warm front stretching from Minnesota to Georgia which abruptly turned into a cold front arching out over the Atlantic Ocean. Another cold front ran from Minnesota to Colorado—cool air moving into Montana, high pressure off the Oregon coast, low pressure in Arizona and New Mexico; high pressure along the Gulf Coast and Virginia, low pressure in Minnesota, cool air sweeping into Pennsylvania, heavy precipitation over a large area of the Mississippi Valley, northwest wind at Elmira fresh to strong, good lapse rate. The newspaper had this one pegged: "Cool temperatures at the higher altitudes indicated a model day for the sailplane flights."

I sat there toward the front of the room in full view of everyone, giving an occasional nod to indicate full comprehension and making copious notes. This was a bit of gamesmanship I had picked up from Stan Smith in Texas the year before. Toward the end of the briefing, I asked a very sophisticated question, nodded again, and wrote furiously for a moment. Then I let the faintest shadow of a smile creep over my face. The effect was tremendous. Half a dozen contestants were shooting worried, furtive glances in my direction. One even tried to peek over and see my notes, but I nonchalantly turned them over and concentrated on Barney Wiggin's *finale*. When he finished, I looked over the charts, made a few corrections to the manuscript, and walked out with Maxey, solemnly talking about the "conditions." I flew twelve miles that day.

The task was a 150 mile out-and-return flight to Norwich, New York. Its direction from Elmira was east-northeast and there was a left crosswind of 23 knots. Having anticipated this takeoff for eleven months, I was so excited I had some difficulty eating a short lunch. *Cirro-Q* and I were towed aloft around noon and after getting to 5000 feet, I set off on course, heavily crabbing into the wind. I had the cruise control chart that John Serafin had made for the 1-23D, but after fifteen minutes, decided the main chore that day was to stay aloft and finish the course, not win a race. My speed between thermals thus became best-glide or 48 miles per hour. Four thermals and twelve miles away from Harris Hill, I found myself over the town of Erin, 35 minutes out, and struggling to get upwind to a good-looking ridge. The thermal which would have taken me there did not materialize, and I sank like a stone, landing in a short field. In the last struggle, there was no time to send a radio message to Jerry, and he went the wrong way. Getting back together took several hours and there was no chance for another try.

Paul Schweizer made the best flight that day, about 110 miles. He was followed by Carris, Coverdale, Stan Smith, Schreder, and Bikle. Maxey was not far behind. Everybody was more or less where he was supposed to be after a day of maddening frustration which convinced everyone aloft he was doing badly in the crosswind that made thermals which were sheared, stalled, and tumbled, but never steady. Everybody was in place except Parker and Thomson. They had left Harris Hill with good altitude, then found not a shred more lift and landed even short of me. Parker rushed back for another try, but could

find nothing better than ridge lift over Harris Hill. Two
of the nation's best, runners-up in the 1954 and 1956 Na-
tionals who had come all the way from California, were
defeated on the first day. They must have wondered if
they should have stayed home with Bob Schnelker.

The morning of July third was clear and cold. We
overheard someone passing our barracks on Harris Hill
mention that it was forty degrees. Paul Bikle hit the floor,
showered, shaved, dressed, ate and returned while the
rest of us were getting up. He wore a floppy hat against
the cold and with his glistening capital dome covered, he
looked incredibly healthy and so youthful he could have
been confused with one of his sons. Parker hit the floor
but was paralyzed by cold. He made a dive into his footlocker and came up with the heavy union suit he had worn
during the International Contest at St. Yan, France, in
1956. All we heard from Maxey was a faint groan. He
slept in a heavy quilted bedroll which was covered with
a pile of woolen blankets, but his feet were pushed out
naked in the air—blue in the cold and with just a trace of
frost on the toes. Bikle jumped up the steps and bounded
over to see him.

"C'mon Maxey, time to get up. You have to fly today."

Two more groans and a little mumbling, followed by
the movements of a prone figure in pain.

"He can't get both eyes open at the same time." Bikle
announced.

There was more struggling under the blankets and
a look of sadness came over Paul Bikle's face. "Poor Max
is out of the contest, he can't get his bedroll unzipped."

Conditions were much weaker the second day and the
task was a race to Tri-City Airport, 42 miles away, straight
downwind, near Binghamton.

After working two thermals, I sank onto a ridge 18
miles out. This time I was right down to the trees, and

60

Jerry could not receive my radio transmissions. The ridge was about a quarter of a mile long, and I flew up and down it for thirty-five minutes, applauding myself at the foresight I had shown in picking it out while there was still time. Then the wind quit, and I landed in a field just beyond a stream at the foot of the ridge. I had flown thirty miles in two days!

July fourth came on weaker still. The sky was covered with a solid overcast and the task was a 100 kilometer triangle to Blue Swan Airport, then to Ithaca and back. For the contestants it was a day of waiting for the sky to open a little. We listened as the public address system cheerily announced to a thousand spectators that it would be exciting for them because they would get to see the sailplanes return at the end of their flights. The spectators did not have to wait for anyone to finish the course. Every once in a while a few ships would go aloft, hunt vainly for a patch of zero sink, and come drifting back to the field like autumn leaves.

I took one tow and landed; not finding either lift or zero sink. My second try was in murky air with a feeling of unreality in the whole sky, like flying in cloudy water. There was an unexpected thermal right off tow, and I climbed slowly up to 4000 feet, just below Schreder, and set off on the first leg. Half way to the turn, I found more lift and squeezed out every foot I could get, then went on to the turn point, sinking only 100 feet a minute. The turn was made at O'Brien's place rather than Blue Swan Airport because of an error on the chart. Then we flew north at maximum-glide speed, 48 miles per hour. Over the ridges, and sinking down to ridgecrest level and then below, hoping, hoping for 32 miles, 50 kilometers. Two flights had to exceed this distance to make it a contest day. Sixty feet above ground, I dropped the nose for a little reserve speed, pulled up over telephone wires and landed in a field of young corn. Twenty-nine miles. For the first time I prayed to be defeated by at least two people. A telephone call gave me the answer on one. Graham Thomson had made thirty-six miles in his RJ-5.

My flight was the second longest of the day. *Cirro-Q* and I were down less than three miles short of making it an official contest day and Graham and I received no points. Only five hundred feet more altitude in the last thermal would have made the difference.

On July fifth, the task was a race to Sidney, 77 miles east-northeast. It was a wonderful soaring day for those who were careful to stay high. Graham Thomson won with an average speed of 75 miles per hour by making use of a cloudstreet. He got under the street and went paddling into the goal more than half an hour ahead of me. A good many sailplanes had already landed on the sunny, green field when I got there, and I followed them down, exalted with the knowledge that I had completed a task in a National Soaring Contest.

July sixth was the first open day. Best flight: Schreder in the new Airmate HP-7; 305 miles to a goal at Logan Airport in Boston. The longest flight was made by Fritz Compton in his old LK. He went 320 miles to Plymouth. Those flights were only the second and third ones over 300 miles in the long soaring history of Elmira.

My takeoff was about three-quarters of the way down the list and a weak thermal took me up 3500 feet above the Hill—not quite enough altitude to risk leaving and with the heavy wind, I did not want to hang on to the thermal too long and not be able to get back. Presently, I decided to leave and fly upwind to better lift. It was not there. We sank to the ground at 500 feet a minute and had to duck back onto the Hill which was now vacant except for Ray Jackson in his white 1-23 and John Bierens in the *Alibi*.

Twenty minutes aloft were followed by twenty minutes on the ground; then came my second tow. The wind had shifted enough to fly ridge lift on the Hill which I started to do, and I worked several thermals up to 3000 feet, only to have them quit and put me back down. Time was getting short because a cirrus overcast had come in from the west and the ground was already shaded. Then the wind abated and my altitude thinned out. I was down only 400 feet above Harris Hill, less than pattern altitude. What should we do? Try it another 20 seconds and risk a downwind landing or one at the County Airport; or quit and burn the rest of the day. This was a National Contest. I hung on.

The thermal came after ten or fifteen seconds, and I started going up, expecting it to quit like the others, but we kept on and on until I had over 5000 feet. Three-quarters of an hour had been spent on the ridge, but we were off now and might hope to get into the sunlight there on the horizon. The first half hour was good, but had no lift that justified flying over 50 miles an hour. Once in a while I put the speed up to 55, but rarely, and I stopped to circle in every scrap of lift, allowing the wind to carry me over the ground.

Our altitude range gradually went up to 4000-6000 feet and slowly we flew toward Binghamton, 55 miles out, where I saw Ray Jackson for the first time since leaving the Hill. He was 500 feet below me in the same thermal and his white 1-23 with copper numbers was beginning to shine because we had worked out of the shaded area at last. He left the thermal ahead of me and flew on very fast. In ten minutes I caught up with him again. He was now 800 feet below me in the same thermal. He left again, flying fast and landed soon afterward, near Binghamton. I went on in conditions which improved a little over the sunny ground, but I was just able to get up to cloudbase.

63

Cirro-Q and I were approaching the Catskill Mountains, homeland of Rip Van Winkle. Their slopes were quiet, lovely, clothed with endless green forest and dotted with well kept farms—a little mysterious as we flew in open sky between mountain slope and cumulus cloud. This was my first mountain crossing in a sailplane, but eastern mountains are not like Arizona ones. The country is populous and there were many fields which would have been suitable for landing in a pinch. I know. Three times during the crossing we were below ridgetop height, within 800 feet of terrain when lift was found. Another minute without lift at any of these points would have brought us down.

After working up to safe altitude the second time, we flew over a mountain valley several miles wide, and I could see that if we made it past a ridge on the far side where the land fell away, I would have effective altitude without further climbing. The sun was getting lower; I had a very late start and had been aloft more than four hours already. At the far side of the valley there was a ridge which ran like the vertical arm of a T up to a mountaintop. This ridge faced the wind. From the summit there were two ridges parallel with the wind—the cap of the T —falling off both upwind and down. The downwind ridge had a notch in it which I hoped to sneak through. I started across the valley toward the distant ridge which might give lift, not quite 2000 feet over the level ground below.

The crossing was made in stable air and tension mounted as the ridge came slowly closer, and we sank toward the floor. At last we made it. There was no lift! Then, after a few seconds it came; first zero sink, then weak lift which kept us a few feet above the ridge crest as it ran at a gentle angle up toward the summit. We were approaching the point where we could make a plunge for the notch in the downwind ridge. Two hundred feet above the crest I went over to the lee side. We sank violently toward the forest below and instantly I made a 180 degree turn and got back in the lift, running again toward the mountaintop. A second try. No heavy sink this time. We have it! And also the thrill of solving a tricky problem in cross-country flight.

On the lee side of the ridge just ascended, we turned and ran parallel to the downwind ridge for half a mile, just even with the height of its crest as it fell away from the summit, then turned left and passed through the notch, flying out over a broad valley far below. I had expected great sink here but none came. Instead, after a few minutes, the last thermal of the day arrived, and I worked out every foot I could get, then headed for the distant side of the valley at my usual best-glide speed. From this height, I could see that on the far side of this new valley, the land fell away again into the Hudson River Valley. The passage looked very long and by the time I was down to 400 feet I had observed a good many landing fields which I thought of using, but just ahead was a tantalizing ridge with another notch in it through which the road passed into the big lower valley. We flew on.

Only 250 feet above terrain we got to this final ridge. The notch was on my left. I banked right to try for a little more altitude from ridge lift, but none was there; not quite zero sink, and a quick turn headed us back for the notch. When we brought it up, we turned and slipped through, clearing the trees by less than a hundred feet. The land again fell away sharply; we crossed a large freeway and were 600 feet above ground in stable air. The last glide took us over a group of large, brick buildings, across from which was a big field of newly mown wheat. At 300 feet, I increased speed, turned onto base leg and final, then went in. Four hours and 58 minutes after takeoff, we were down again when the sun was almost touching the last ridge we had crossed. We were at Coxsackie, New York,

21 miles south of Albany, 158 miles from Harris Hill and just two miles west of the Hudson River.

July eighth decided the contest. Weather looked bad and the task of the day was a speed dash to Syracuse. Around 11 o'clock the sky was almost clear for a short interval, but nobody used this opportunity to go aloft. By noon it was overcast again and the early flights of Bikle, Schreder, and others who tried were very short. Stan Smith went up at just the right moment to catch an ominous looking wave which appeared as a writhing black line in the gray sky. He flew with brilliance and daring, sometimes in rain which reduced visibility to zero, and landed at the goal. Del Miller made it a contest day by going 41 miles.

I made every possible mistake, but still glided 15 miles. After leaving Harris Hill, I headed on course in strange air that kept my sinking rate down to 100 feet a minute. I knew there was an airport at Montour Falls, just below the southern extremity of Seneca Lake, 15 miles out, and headed for it at 46 miles per hour, less than best-glide speed, reasoning that the tailwind might flatten out my glide a trace. We flew in glassy air, sinking down to hilltop level, then well below. The lake was getting very close, and south of the waterline I saw a great field of cat-tails over six feet deep, but no airport where the chart promised one. The country all about was virtually unlandable—forest, vineyards, and areas of tightly packed houses. Four hundred feet were left and still no airport. Had it been abandoned or closed since my air chart was published? Things like that happen. Then at 350 feet it materialized right where it was supposed to be; marvelously disguised by the color of a sod strip under the dark overcast sky. A base leg and final approach brought us down, and within twenty minutes, Graham Thomson brought the RJ-5 down onto the same field.

Fifteen miles, and oddly there were only four or five longer flights that day. If Del Miller had flown ten miles less, it would not have been a contest day. If I had made two and a half miles more on July fourth, it *would* have been a contest day. If—but then, that is why you go to contests.

We had supper that night at Howard Johnson's Restaurant and were joined by Maxey and the Prues. They told us about the landing damage suffered by Hoverman and Parker. Lyle Maxey ordered and ate in silence. I had seen him go aloft on his first flight in the *Jenny Mae* in Texas the year before—1000 points for best flight of the day; I had seen him round the first turn on his last day in Texas—1000 points; over 8500 out of a possible 9000. Only nine miles today. The same pilot: a champion undone.

July ninth. Pilots' meeting was on while there was the usual heavy solid overcast, and bitter complaints went up when the contest committee called a 200 kilometer task to Endicott, Courtland, and return to Harris Hill. Most of the pilots ought to have known better. The overcast broke and the weather turned out exactly as Barney Wiggin said it would: excellent fair weather cumulus with a wind of 20 to 25 knots at west-northwest. Apparently a hole developed at the first turn that day when several people were there and it brought down some good pilots, including Dick Schreder. At the time I was there, things were easy except for the powerful cross-headwind. Some cloudstreets formed, pointing back toward Elmira, and the leaders took advantage of this condition so they had to crab only thirty degrees into the wind on the second leg instead of sixty. At midafternoon a vast hole in the weather blew in and dropped everyone on the ground at almost the same time. An hour and a half later, conditions were good once again and if there had been a ridge around Courtland on which to stay aloft, several pilots might have finished the triangle.

Soaring

Fritz Compton was the hero of the day. Flying in conditions which gave a distinct advantage to high penetration aircraft, he used more than one cloudstreet to gain on the crosswind, and flew the last glide, right to the ground, with perfection and courage. He tied Paul Bikle for 1000 points. Even though I was three miles back of them in second place, I had the satisfaction of landing *Cirro-Q* ahead of both Maxey and Thomson, a thrill best understood by someone who has flown a Baby Albatross against those gentlemen in Texas.

My last 3000 feet of altitude had been sacrificed by an endless downdraft as I tried to get upwind to a ridge. The landing was on a precipitous hillside where the slope was over 25 degrees, just beyond a break in the ground where the hill climbed at a solid 45 degree angle. Going up such an incline, my landing roll was only 60 feet. On the way down to a farmhouse, I passed the angle in the hill which left *Cirro-Q* out of sight when I was less than 200 feet away.

The lower part of the hill was so steep I had trouble getting down, but presently made it and walked into a farmyard with the usual landing-witness papers which pilots must have signed after every landing away from the contest field to verify their performance for scoring.

I met a farmer who seemed a little doubtful at first when I told him I had just landed a sailplane up on his hill, but he was easily convinced and quickly signed my landing statement. Then he took me into his house and introduced me to his wife. She was quiet, sullen, and very deaf so the conversation was tiring and had to be shouted at a level of many decibels. In a few minutes it became obvious that I had aroused her suspicions, and she took me for a city slicker who was out to foreclose on the ranch.

"I just landed a sailplane up on your hill. I'm in the National Soaring Contest at, ..." I began before she interrupted.

"How's that? You'll have to talk louder. Can't hear a thing you say."

"I said I just landed a sailplane up on your hill. I'm in the soaring contest at Elmira. When we land away from the field we have to get landing witnesses to sign these landing statements. Your husband signed this one for me." It had been a long time since I had shouted like that and my voice began to feel gravelly.

"What's a sailplane? Never heard of it."

"A glider, a high performance glider," I screamed pleasantly. "I say I just landed one up on your hill and . . ."

"You mean like a airplane what doesn't have no propeller?"

"That's right," I yelled, finally beginning to feel the establishment of rapport.

"You tryin' to tell me you landed one of them things up there?" she nodded her head toward the hill.

At the back of their living room were high windows, but the hill was so steep I could just see the break where the incline was more gradual, beyond which I had gone down. Looking through those windows, even though I just landed up there, I had to admit to myself the whole story began to seem fantastically improbable. Maybe this realization showed on my face because I noticed the farmer began looking at me with narrow appraisal.

"Yes," I shouted belligerently. "I can show you my aircraft if you want to see it. Also, I would like to use your telephone to call my crewchief if I may. He's going to come after me with a car and trailer."

Just then a little girl burst into the living room. She began shouting with great excitement.

"Grandma, Grandma—an airplane just crashed up on your hill. Did you see it?"

I could not help being a little smug. "There! You see!"

"Ah that girl can really think 'em up. I ain't goin' to sign no paper. I never saw no airplane."

"But your granddaughter just told you that . . ."

"Ah, her! Last week she told me she seen a herd of crocodiles runnin' down the road."

I was defeated. There was nothing to do but ask the farmer if I could use his telephone. He gave me permission, and I called Don Ryon at Harris Hill to relay my position to Jerry Robertson. Then I stomped out and went back up their hill. I looked down once or twice and both the farmer and his wife stood in the yard watching me climb.

When I got back to *Cirro-Q* I sat down in the grass and waited for two hours. The narrow valley I looked across was not unusual but had the pristine loveliness of upper New York State. The clouds I had flown under were disappearing at the eastern horizon. From time to time a car would drive leisurely along the road below, which wound its way along the stream. The slopes of my hill, and the one across from the stream were in bright yellow sunlight which imperceptibly changed into a deep golden color as the afternoon wore on; and the clouds which had been just barely visible on the western horizon when I had been going down came over now. I watched this from under *Cirro-Q's* uptilted wing and knew I was a lucky man; for I lived in the age of time-saving machines which allow no time, the age of efficiency which is too efficient for much living, the age of organization which is too organized to allow solitude—almost by accident I had been allowed those hours on a hill near Courtland.

When I thought there had been nearly enough time for Jerry to drive up from Elmira, I went down to the road again and waited for him. In twenty minutes he arrived. I took Jerry in and introduced him to my farmer friend after warning him not to converse with the wife

70

unless he wanted to risk permanent strain on his vocal cords. The farmer's wife gazed at my station wagon and trailer as if they were a hallucination. I am certain it never occurred to her there was a modicum of truth in anything I had said, and now she must begin to wonder.

The little girl was there, shouting at the top of her lungs to Grandmother; and a young man arrived with a big tractor. We asked if they knew of a road leading up onto their hill. The young man did, although he said it was too muddy to be passable. Then, with courtly hospitality, he offered to pull the station wagon and trailer up the road with his tractor.

Three quarters of an hour later, *Cirro-Q* was de-rigged and back on its trailer. The young man with the tractor had not exaggerated. The trail was rough and so muddy that he even had to pull us down the hill. Before we left, he signed my landing card, and I even managed to get the farmer's bride to put her name on it—the greatest triumph of all.

The final day was open and had a forecast for good distance weather. Since I had made the second longest flight the day before, my standing had come up, and I had one of the first choices for take-off time. I decided to go early.

Rushing madly to get everything ready, I was airborne at 11:00 o'clock with a sealed barograph ticking behind my head, no food, and a goal 230 miles away in the state of Virginia. Sailplanes were circling at 1300 feet in weak lift, but I took all 2000 feet before releasing. Almost immediately I found weak lift and made the insane decision to hold on to it in the bristling north wind. The lift held up just long enough to put me beyond range of Harris Hill, then quit dead. In steady sink, I went down as we flew over the west end of Elmira, never making a turn until we were over the ridge at South Mountain,

Soaring

seven miles away from the Hill and still in sight of Jerry
Robertson who was watching through field glasses. The
ridge soaring was easy. Occasionally, a weak thermal came
along and took me up two or three hundred feet. Other
sailplanes joined me. The RJ-5 went over a scant 1000
feet above, and I was worried when Graham Thomson
headed for the forest country to the south.

Cirro-Q and I flew back and forth in endless beats.
A feeling of absolute security came over me and kept
growing stronger even though my wingtip was often only
a span away from the trees. Thermals with strong lift
would become violent sink when we had gained three
or four hundred feet and always we had to go back to
the ridge. When the overcast broke, my optimism increased
for a get-away and a long flight. Then wind abated, and
four sailplanes landed at the foot of the ridge within five
minutes of each other. I was the first one down after soaring the ridge for one hour and thirty-five minutes. We
made only seven miles and twenty-nine points that day.

I was too hungry, disgusted, and defeated to make
another try. For me it was over: I had finished in eigh-
teenth place in my second National Contest. That day
Paul Bikle soared to Cape May, New Jersey, around 240
miles, and landed on the beach at the last possible tip of
land for his second consecutive day with 1000 points.

The following afternoon, I took the flight examination
for a commercial glider license from Bernie Carris. On the
final spot landing Dick Schreder passed me in his HP-7,
wingtip to wingtip, not six feet away. Neither of us had
seen the other on that approach. Jerry Robertson and I
looked down the field to where the HP-7 had stopped,
then de-rigged *Cirro-Q* and loaded it carefully on the
trailer for our long trip home. That evening, we went to
the awards banquet which is the climax at the end of every
National Soaring Contest.

72

CHAPTER 8

The Crash of the HP-7

Next morning Jerry Robertson and I were getting ready to leave Harris Hill. The new copy of ARIZONA AIR CURRENTS arrived in the mail and ran the story of Dave Mead's TG-3 crash in Tucson. It was a bad one. Dave had been working all afternoon in the sun without a hat or water. When he finally got airborne, he passed out from heat stroke a few seconds after releasing from automobile tow and spun into the ground from three hundred feet, destroying the ship. Dave's feet and ankles were crushed and the legs were splintered up to his knees. The Schweizer structure absorbed an enormous crash force, and the seat belt and shoulder straps held or the accident would have been fatal.

Twenty minutes after reading this report, we were almost finished packing when someone who had been on the telephone in contest headquarters brought us the somber report about Dick Schreder's beautiful white HP-7.

The HP-7 was going home by aero-tow and maintaining radio contact with its towplane which was carrying passengers. They took off and flew west out of Elmira, climbing steadily, past cloudbase, 4000 feet above terrain, past 6000, 7000, 9000, toward the upper air where a sailplane cannot go unless it is towed, where the air is flat and smooth, above cloud, and it is easier to fly on a long cross-country tow.

They were off course to the south and the pilot in the tow ship headed for a deep notch in a building cumulus cloud. This was questioned, both in the towplane and by the pilot in the HP-7, but the towpilot went on without a turn. Driven by a strange feeling of competition? Must he outclimb the cloud? As they approached cloud, the race to outclimb the rising gorge became very near. The towpilot, using full throttle, raised the nose of his aircraft higher and higher to increase his rate of climb. Speed fell off. The pilot in the sailplane frantically asked for more power; he asked for speed—he was very near the stall. The towplane dropped its nose a little and at once they were going through a narrow canyon of mist; then instantly it closed about them and both aircraft were immersed in luminous white vapor and thrown around in heavy turbulence. The pilot in the sailplane had his electric turn-and-bank instrument on; he felt a violent pull downward which vanished as quickly as it started—then he sensed the towrope had broken.

In every direction, turbulence and blinding white, so thick he could not see his wingtips. A glance at the panel showed the turn-and-bank needle pegged, the ball of the instrument was as far as it could go the other way—the sigh of airnoise in the cockpit quickly turned into a whistle and grew louder. He knew he was diving.

The towplane, thrown over on its back, shuddered and went into a spin. After many turns from which the pilot could not recover, the plane fell out the side of the cloud, and suddenly they were in clear air, where the pilot recovered his level, upright attitude, and all those in the towplane were now looking behind at the boiling white mass they had left. They knew they would see nothing, but could not help looking back and with eyes of frozen fascination, they saw the broken towrope, without a steel eye at the far end, unburdened now, dangling free.

In the sailplane, there was a fight against panic as the mind spread terrible seconds into what seemed minutes. He remembered to use gentle control movements and tried to straighten his turn by rudder pressure while the whistle of air changed into a roar, then into a howling, buffeting scream. The cloud grew darker, and he knew he was getting near the bottom. No feeling of speed, even though he was diving at hundreds of miles per hour — only a blind, gray world of crashing sound—then he burst through cloudbase and saw ground only a little way down; and instinctively, convulsively, with an agony of terror, he pulled the stick back as far as it would come—an explosion like a cannon right at his ear, and he looked to see the wing gone: took a smashing blow on the shoulder and another on the head, and half the other wing had gone; then an instant pull to get off the harness and open the canopy—a tearing of heavy air at his body as he was free, then a plunge at the chest with his right hand—but he caught the fastener buckle in the middle instead of getting the ripcord ring on left side. Then there wasn't anything more.

An eye on the ground might have looked up, attracted by the sound of two explosions, and seen an unguided, white bomb falling; something coming out of it with the unbelievable appearance of a human figure, then two other

75

white things falling—one spinning as it fell, with the unlikeliness of an arm falling free of the body; and separate metallic crunches as the pieces struck earth.

The towplane landed in a field across from where the sailplane had fallen. The pilot got out, ran across the road and saw. Then he burst into tears and stumbled to the ground: "I made a terrible mistake today I made a terrible mistake today I made a terrible mistake today."

The Schreders were called back from the end of their honeymoon trip to the scene of the crash. When Jerry and I got to the field where the HP-7 had gone in, we saw Angie Schreder and the scores of morbidly curious—the parts of a white wing lying in a field in the distance, with FAA officials investigating; the fuselage in a barn with its nose crumpled like an accordion, the smashed Peravia, the unopened parachute. There was nothing we could do. After saying goodbye, we drove on west through the rolling country as evening came on.

CHAPTER 9

Beyond the Canadian River

Jerry and I settled down to the second half of our seven thousand mile trip and after the way of soaring people, we talked of nothing but sailplanes and the sky. As dusk was turning into night, we drove along the bank of a silent river and when I pulled on the headlights, a cloud of insects flew up in front of the car like the sparks of a ghostly fire. I kept looking in the mirror to see the image of *Cirro-Q*—key to the magic in the life of any soaring pilot, his own sailplane.

We were depressed. All the glory and frustration of the Meet were now history; a new champion was going home. I remembered my landing in a wet, grass field at the end of my first cross-country flight out of Elmira, after thinking for a desperate moment I had lost my sailplane. I thought of the wonderful day when I had completed my

Soaring

first task in a Contest with the landing at Sidney after
finishing a 77 mile goal race, and having a can of beer
that Bill Coverdale had brought out to that sunny, grass
field under a sky full of cumulus cloud that must have
been made in Paradise; and the long anxious flight over
the Catskill Mountains, and the beautiful afternoon spent
on the hill at Courtland. Now it was past. We had said
goodbye to all the pilots and crews; the Contest was over.

On July 18th, we were at the Flying W Ranch in
Cedar Hill, Texas, where we had spent the night with the
Wibergs and had finished washing and rigging *Cirro-Q*.
The plan was to make another attempt at Golden C Distance. Jerry was putting on the final touches; I had finished a sandwich and was in the shower. Temperature
was over 100, humidity high, and the beautiful cumulus
clouds of Texas were growing stronger by the minute.
A goal had been set north of Wichita and the tow began
at 11:48, after June Wiberg had spent an hour and a
half on the telephone locating a towpilot. I released at
1800 feet and made a dive to 1700 to notch the barogram,
found lift and set off.

Only 250 feet per minute altitude gained here, guess
the big lift is under that cloud to the west . . . . 250 fpm
here too, let's try that one over Grand Prairie Airport, it
is really big . . . . 250 fpm. What is this, a joke? You're in
Texas. Notice how the clouds don't have much vertical
development? 250 feet per minute again. The fourth thermal in a row. Wichita is out. So north we go at the speed
of a Bowlus, 20 miles an hour plus a good 15 knot tailwind,
35 mph; up to 5000 feet, down to 3000, up to five, down
to three. The lapse rate is moderate, and it is hot even at
5000; I can't reach cloudbase at 6000, and my hangover
from the party the night before with the Wibergs and
E. J. Reeves is coming back. Is this supposed to be fun?

78

Down below, slowly past the beloved landmarks of the 23rd National Soaring Contest: Amon Carter Field, Grapevine Reservoir, Denton, Sanger, Gainesville, the Red River, Marietta. My stomach is much better now and so is the lift, up to 333 fpm and we have come a hundred miles. Look out now, let's pay attention to what we're doing—it's not considered intelligent to circle in 500 fpm down—there, that's getting better. That thermal must have been caved in on one side.

The little village down there must be Elmore City, one hundred and thirty miles out, where I took the Baby Albatross last summer and got let down. Not today though, still 6000 feet high and looking up. There is Paul's Valley, and sure enough, the Canadian River below the horizon. It flows just south of Oklahoma City. Never got quite far enough to see it last summer. This is getting interesting; 157 miles at Elmira is my best, and down there below, only seven miles ahead, is the 160 mile mark on my chart. What's this? 500 fpm lift all the way around the circle? We soared up and did not turn on course again until the lift weakened at 8100.

Let's see now. For 500 fpm climb, you're supposed to go 85 miles per hour according to John Serafin's chart. 85? You don't *quite* have Golden Distance in the bag. O. K., 75. Down and down to 7000, 6000, 5000, 4000; slowing down gradually, then back to best glide-angle speed again, going down still. 3000 feet.

What happened? The clouds are all dissolving, and the air is sinking everywhere. How many miles of it have we flown through? Just west of Norman Airport, we are down only 1200 feet above the ground and at this rate of sink, we should make about 183 miles. Only four miles less than Golden Distance; what an ending! Shall I try it over the airport? There might be a thermal over the big asphalt mat, and at least a good landing place. No, let's take it over 180 miles. Continue straight ahead on course. What now? Zero sink? Impossible, but here it is! With the tailwind, each four minutes of this will add a mile. Maybe you aren't dead yet.

The battle began: Zero sink became slow, patchy lift. There was the shudder of stall warning; sink, nose down, tighten your bank, shift the pattern again, lift, nose up, now push nose down again; lift, sink, lift, change bank— every muscle tense; how is the altimeter? 200 feet up. Tap it: 300 up; let's check it every circle . . . . 100 feet gained on this one . . . . 100 feet again . . . . No good this time, but here's a big chunk of lift, 100 feet again . . . We are up a thousand feet above low point. Oh no! 500 fpm down! Quick now, let's find it. A desperate search is made through the area. Here's the lift again, but how did it get way over here? We lost 300 feet in the sink, but now we are getting it back again very nicely. 3400 feet above sea level. 2,000 feet above terrain. The clouds have all gone to pot. Can we get up to 4000? No, we can't get to the moon, but we're still going up . . . . 4000! We made it!

Muscles easing off; relax now. The lift is easier. No longer patchy; getting stronger—150 fpm; now 200 fpm. Forget everything but the climb; figure glide angles later. We kept soaring very carefully and the climb went on.

7100 feet. How did we make it? There are no good clouds left up here or anywhere else. Thirty-five minutes have been spent in the most difficult climb I ever made with success, and we have drifted north as far as Will Rogers Field, in the southwest quadrant of Oklahoma City. From here we could easily dive for Tulakes Airport, which Wally Wiberg thought should be my goal. It would have been good for a Diamond. Where shall we go now? Guthrie looks good. A check of distance on the chart— 27 miles away. Let's enjoy this last glide; there is a good

JUNE AND WALLY WIBERG. *He is ready for takeoff in his sailplane Lil Dogie.*

RUTH PETRY AND BOB SPARLING. *She is at the controls of a Piper Pacer getting ready to make an aero-tow.*

airport there. What a difference from some of the fields at Elmira!

Before takeoff, I always set the aircraft clock on high noon. It now registered 5:48. I wanted to stretch it out for a six-hour flight and Guthrie would be easy to reach if I reduced my speed to minimum sink: 45 miles per hour indicated. Six o'clock came and passed. I watched speed-boats make their insect-like wakes on two big ponds just south of Guthrie. Then we set up a long, lazy pattern, riding on clouds of exaltation. The landing was six hours and four minutes after takeoff. I got out with a left knee so stiff that for a time I could hardly walk, but inside I was still soaring.

Previous distance flights in Texas had carried 108 miles, 36, and 130 miles. In Elmira, 127 miles, 157, and 7 miles. The crewing was brilliant. I called Arlington, Texas, and got Ruth Nephew who had agreed to serve at contest headquarters that day. She had already received a crew call from Oklahoma City, put through by Jerry Robertson and June Wiberg. Less than five minutes after I went out to the main road, they drove up with the trailer. We were 221 airline miles away from takeoff point, 34 miles beyond the Gold C Distance Leg requirement of 300 kilometers, after a flight made without radio contact. It was a fitting end to my soaring odyssey of 1957. *Cirro-Q* and I had flown Golden Distance.

CHAPTER 10

My Golden C

After flying the Distance Leg in Texas, it almost became an obsession to finish the requirement for my Golden C pin with an altitude gain of 3000 meters (9843 feet). The Golden wreath beckoned; it was a siren call, the mark of an advanced soaring pilot.

In August, the desert air around Phoenix tends to be comparatively stable, and there is danger of heat stroke during ground handling in a closed cockpit sailplane. For this reason, I decided to try for the altitude gain in Prescott, where the soaring was said to be fabulous, and I knew of a flight which had carried up to 18,700 feet. There was no towplane there, so it was necessary to get a long piece of towcable at Rittenhouse Field. Captain and Sally Schmid went to Prescott with me the first weekend for an attempt at soaring from automobile tow. The sky clouded over solidly and *Cirro-Q* was never taken off its trailer. The following weekend, I went up with Jerry Robertson and Beebo, my German Shepherd. We got to Prescott in the middle of the night and got up shortly after dawn. By a tremendous effort on the part of Jerry Robertson, Bob Sparling, Joe Vest, and myself, I got in twenty-one minutes of flying that day.

Twenty-one minutes! I had spent four hours in the summer sun at Rittenhouse Field untangling a thousand-foot piece of armored towcable for those flights; another hour had gone into rolling it onto a telephone cable drum. Five hundred miles of trailing in those two weekends for twenty-one minutes of flying over Chino Valley.

By midmorning, we had rigged *Cirro-Q* and laid out the cable so Jerry could drive on the road which ran straight for over a mile from starting position of the car. A thousand feet away from the station wagon, at the sailplane end of the cable, we had picked an area free of rocks and bushes where the ground was fairly smooth and promised little diffiiculty for my takeoff run which is generally accomplished in less than a hundred yards with automobile tow. The engine was weakened by altitude and on his first try, Jerry had trouble getting the car up to speed. I could gain only 150 feet of altitude. The landing was less than a mile away from takeoff point, beside a water tank for cattle. We then towed *Cirro-Q* behind the car to a new location for the next try and made out a little better. Peak altitude the second time was 350 feet. Noon came and passed; another long ground tow behind the car to a third location; a break for lunch; an hour spent planning the tow and laying out the cable, while overhead, as the day wore on, there were towering cumuli which were so beautiful they might have cracked the heart of a saint.

This time, the car had to go down a slight hill, and

the tow began from a position in which the car was out of sight from the sailplane at first, necessitating some complicated hand signals. Half a mile ahead of the point where the car began its tow, the road sharply turned right and passed over a cattle guard between heavy fence posts. Once airborne, it would immediately be necessary to swing out left of the car so the cable would be lined up with the road after the turn was made and not snag in the fence. Jerry drove; Bob Sparling was handling the cable from the back of the car, and Joe Vest managed the hand signals and wingtip running.

The tow started, and I got airborne sooner than before since the car was going down hill. A hundred feet up in the air, I brought the car into sight, began pulling to the left and climbing very fast. At 400 feet I had all the cable off the ground and lined up with the second part of the road; then Jerry rounded the turn at fifty miles an hour. At 500 feet *Cirro-Q* began porpoising, and I was grateful for the advice of Bob Sparling who had told me how to dampen this kind of oscillation with anticipatory elevator control. 600 feet, then no more. Quite good for only a thousand feet of towcable. I released and with the wings unloaded from downward pull of the cable, we zoomed up to 700 feet. There was very weak lift and ten minutes of soaring got us up to 800 feet; but it was under a thin cirrus overcast that had come in. The lift failed, and we did not get away. Soon we landed close to where the car had stopped and got ready for a last attempt. Even that late it still seemed like a good day for Golden C altitude.

The final attempt was made crosswind on the narrow road. Bob Sparling asked me if I thought it was safe in the brisk wind, because there would be no rudder control during the first part of the tow. I did not think there was anything to worry about. After three quarters of an hour, the cable was laid out again in the new direction. The tow began. *Cirro-Q* made a left turn which I could not control with rudder; the pull of the towcable abruptly stopped it, and we headed too far right, again uncontrollable. A writhing oscillation began, like horizontal porpoising, which could not be controlled and which used up the whole width of the road. As the speed increased, each wave got bigger. After changing direction six times, I released the towcable while heading for the shallow ditch. We jumped it and stopped with a crunching sound that made me fear damage.

My flying was over for that day. *Cirro-Q's* newly repaired tailwheel was almost broken off; a wingtip had been scraped and there was damage to the wooden keel. That same day, Paul Bikle flew his 1-23 to a world speed record in California.

On Sunday, the first of September, I trailed *Cirro-Q* out to Rittenhouse Field, southeast of Chandler, Arizona, and got airborne behind Don's towplane at 3:30 in the afternoon. The towplane looked very good after the recent weekend in Prescott. That flight carried to 9000 feet above terrain, and we soared over Superstition Mountain. The forecast of the morrow's Labor Day weather looked even better, and I got to the field early. The Cinema and Baby Albatross were both aloft when I took my tow a little after noon with two barographs running behind my head.

I released at 1700 feet and made a dive to 1500 to notch the barograms. The towpilot had found a wonderful thermal for me to start the flight, and I quickly soared up to 5500 feet above the field before lift weakened; then I headed for the happy hunting ground of the mountain to the north where tall cumulus clouds indicated powerful updrafts. On the way over to the road, half way between Apache Junction and Florence Junction, there was no lift but plenty of strong sink. The ridge where Chuck Schmid had gone down in the Pratt-Read was in sight, and I got nervous as we sank below the top of Superstition Mountain—that strange, haunted, symmetrical structure that looks like a futuristic and heroic temple from the Orient, with overhanging cliffs a thousand feet high that seem to emit haze and will not give up the mystery of the Lost Dutchman's Mine.

Finally, we got a strong thermal which took us up almost to 9000 feet. Above Superstition there was widespread lift, strong patchy lift intermingled with downdrafts—far below the clouds. We ultimately attained cloudbase over the mountain under a series of spent, motheaten cumuli. Two or three good ones had developed to the west over Apache Junction and some bigger ones were in the distance toward Superior. I took the direction of Apache Junction and soon got under a strong cloud. Lift in this area weakened at 11,300 feet A. T., just a little short of Golden Altitude. Then I spotted a bigger cloud two miles west with fine vertical development. Sink between clouds lowered us to the base as we reached it and then circled up again. The next seventeen minutes were in lift which varied from weak sink to very strong climb and I tried to stay in the best part as well as possible with shallow turns in patchy visibility caused by a mist wet enough that my yarn yaw indicator lay down on the canopy like a wash rag. At high point the altimeter read 13,700 feet above terrain. 12,200 feet of altitude had been gained.

The summit of Four Peaks was far below; even Roosevelt Lake seemed near from that height—it was a time of glory, with sunlight and cloud and clear air between. My oxygen mask had been on for over half an hour and suddenly I began to feel very tired. After fifteen minutes of bliss at that altitude, *Cirro-Q* and I flew back home at 120 miles an hour and lost the final height cavorting with acrobatics.

Soaring

Golden C complete! And a new Arizona Soaring Association altitude record: 15,250 feet above sea level; 12,200 feet gained, over 2300 feet more than the requirement. Counting automobile tows in Prescott, the flight was made on my tenth try for Golden Altitude.

CHAPTER 11

Tombstone

In 1958, the spring season began early. I checked the weather for Sunday, March 23rd; it looked good. Convection was to be strong; the wind from north-northwest to west-northwest at 20 knots, perfect for a Diamond Goal Flight to Douglas, over 210 miles away from Turf Paradise, our local airstrip which paralled a horse race track northwest of Phoenix, where we had received permission to move our operation. Flight preparations were under way by Saturday night.

On Sunday, I was up at 6:20 with a date to meet Bertha and Marcel Godinat by 9:00 o'clock. Chet Howard, our towpilot who had his own biplane, was going to be at the field by 10:15. Jerry Robertson also came along, and we made a new speed record washing down *Cirro-Q*. Final preparations; rigging, sealing the Peravia, and load-

89

ing up took another hour and a half. I had too much gear
along. Food, coffee, an extra jacket, charts, kneeboard
pen, cruise control curves, and finally my new Swiss knife
which Marcel thought I might need.

Takeoff was at 11:50 and lift began at something over
500 feet a minute, up to cloudbase at 7000 feet. I waved
goodbye to Don Barnard in the TG-3 and headed southeast
on course, giving my crew a call on the Skycrafter radio.
Conditions were tremendous, and we ran 80 miles per hour
between the first thermals. It took longer than I had expected to get over Camelback Mountain, but I got there
after deciding that my altitude range for the day's flying
would be somewhere between 8000 and 5000 feet. Over
the mountain I saw a newspaper which had been carried
aloft almost up to my altitude.

South of Scottsdale, I looked for the first time at
cloud shadows to see them racing toward Douglas. The
surface wind at Turf Paradise Race Track had been in
the wrong direction by the hefty margin of 170 degrees,
but I knew this was only a local condition. I had checked
the meteorology thoroughly. At first glance, I was satisfied
with the wind aloft; then I looked again, blinked, rubbed
my eyes, and looked hard again. The wind was almost
directly out of the south at what appeared to be 20 knots.
The weather office had forecast all other conditions ac-
curately, but had missed the wind vector by 135 degrees.
Half way between Scottsdale and Mesa, the clouds on my
course had all but disappeared, and by the time I got to
Chandler, my speed was cut in half by weaker lift. Prospects were dimming.

Jerry called me on the radio from the car and sug-
gested a goal-and-return flight to Tucson. It seemed possible, but I was flying for a Diamond and did not want
to abandon my Goal. The station wagon and trailer caught

up with me just beyond Chandler and began the leisurely drive south, with frequent stops to wait for me. The rest of the day they had me in sight, and once or twice I saw them on the road below.

Two hours and fifteen minutes out, I was near Coolidge Airport, not quite within gliding range, over dubious landing terrain and in trouble for the first time. We were only 1000 feet above ground. I worked out of that hole and went on slowly, pressing toward Desert Peak. My course was altered now to keep *Cirro-Q* over better landing country and on the north side of Desert Peak we were down again to 1400 feet, looking over the fields. Then came a good thermal, and we soared up well over the mountain top. I flew past the summit and caught another lift on the south side. Up again at 6500 feet, I set course for Redrock, halfway between Picacho and Marana Airbase. There was a big hole in the lift here, and we flew on and on, sinking. Finally the altimeter read 2400 feet, only five hundred above ground. I radioed the crew to keep me in sight; the flight was just about over. Then a weak lift! Five minutes of desperate soaring gained us 300 feet before the lift quit, and I went back over the field I was going to use. New lift appeared. Generally in this position you get 100 foot lift in the first half of a circle, and 250 fpm down in the second half. To my surprise, this time the second half gave 300 up. We shifted pattern into the better lift and the flight was saved. In twenty minutes we had safe altitude again. The headwind abated and my loss of distance while drifting north during the climb was not close to the altitude I had gained.

I foresaw that by using a technique Dick Johnson calls austerity gliding, there was a faint possibility of making Tucson, still 40 miles away, even though it was 4:30 in the afternoon. You fly at best-glide speed and use every shred of lift to the maximum. I knew if we got low again after 5:00 p. m., the flight would be ended and the heavy overgrowth in the terrain ahead made landing prospects there look dismal. This worked out better than hoped for and up at altitude the lift was good—300 feet a minute. Slowly, we flew on, then came the last thermal of the day, fifteen miles out of Gilpin Airport in the northwest corner of the city. This lift carried up to a point where it would be easy to make Gilpin, and there was even a possibility of making the downtown airport, another ten miles away. I headed on course at fifty miles an hour indicated, slowly converting my altitude into distance. The sun got lower. At 5500 feet, 3300 above ground, the impossible happened. We flew into another thermal! It carried us clear back up to 8000 feet, close to the high point for the day. Now the big Tucson Municipal Airport would be easy to make, and I instructed the crew to go there and wait for me.

All over Tucson there was lift. It was the first time I had ever flown in an evening thermal, and our altitude went up to the highest point of the day, 8840 feet above sea level, and when we reached the Tucson Municipal Field, it was over a mile straight down; six hours after takeoff. My knees were wobbly, feet were freezing, and hindquarters ached from cold and lack of circulation.

Two Arizona Soaring Association records had been set. Distance: 123 miles, and duration. When the sun went down, we were still almost a mile high. A decision was made to end the flight before darkness fell, and when we were cleared for landing the strip lights were already on. The flight had lasted six hours and fifty-five minutes.

My next try was on Sunday, April 13th. The wind aloft was quite weak, but in the right direction and a flight to a Diamond Goal at Bisbee-Douglas International Airport seemed indicated. We had to use my Piper for a towplane that day, and it was almost noon when we were airborne in a sky filled with promising cumuli. Newlywed Bob and Dottie Moore crewed for me.

The initial climb was moderate, but not discouraging. Thirty-five minutes after takeoff, I left Turf Paradise with 8400 feet and from there to Camelback Mountain, I made rapid progress in good lift. Then things went bad. There were no clouds over the valley; I began to get lower and had to slow down. One hour out I was over Mesa, only twenty miles from Turf Paradise, and Bob Moore caught up with me. After two hours, I was southeast of Chandler, just forty miles from takeoff, grinding round and round in 100 fpm lift to keep airborne, low enough that landing was a definite possibility. Then we flew over the Santan Mountains, a little gingerly at first because of the low altitude. I thought a little about the scrape I had been in at Coolidge three weeks before, but now I was almost certain I could get out to one of the big fields if an emergency landing became necessary.

Then things picked up fast. We got a strong thermal and went back up over 8000 for the first time since leaving Camelback Mountain and headed out with good speed. Presently, Florence came up and a broken cloudstreet was observed ahead. I radioed Bob to make all possible speed toward Tucson because things were boiling. The next hour we flew the biggest conditions of my life, with lift averaging a solid 1000 feet a minute, and we made 65 miles.

Three hours out, 105 miles behind me, 104 miles to the Goal. Over Mount Lemmon a snowstorm was in progress, and other storms were east of Tucson. They were obviously spent and even with 11,000 feet of altitude, it was going to be difficult getting around the dead areas they had left. We flew over the Catalinas, just a few hundred feet over the boulders at ridgetop, then across the valley east of Tucson, sinking all the way. I was in a jam by the time we pulled up the western slopes of Mica Mountain and tried to find ridge lift. None was about. Where lift should have been according to the wind, there was heavier than average sink. We flew on across that mountain to a valley twenty miles southeast of Tucson where I expected nothing. I was down only 2300 feet above terrain and thought the flight was probably nearing an end when we found a thermal which boosted us up over 8000 feet again. I informed the crew by radio, and we all headed for Benson. A second thermal took us almost up to 11,000 feet near Benson. Even though this was seven thousand feet above terrain in a 30 to 1 glide-angle sailplane, it was becoming obvious that reaching the goal would be very difficult. Ahead there was a vast hole in cloud development that extended clear to Mexico. Above mountains to the right and left of my course, well out of gliding range, there were good cumulus clouds, but the valley ahead was open. We flew into the gauntlet and began sinking 400 feet a minute steadily.

Benson and St. David went by. Some good fields appeared below me when I had no more than a thousand feet of altitude left, but I had seen one tiny cumulus, hardly bigger than a large aircraft, form and dissipate over the valley, and seeing it kept hope alive. Then for a moment I got something a little better than zero sink. It vanished. We flew south over some badlands hoping the dry knolls would kick up lift. Nothing. Still farther south I got lift. It was the fascinating challenge of weak, difficult lift, which so often gets better with altitude; over bad terrain, late in the day—a dare to finish the long flight under tough conditions. Twenty minutes of frantic soaring produced some 1200 feet of new altitude, but it also drifted us along course to within a mile of Tombstone, over shaggy country which was visibly getting higher as we slowly went up, thus reducing the effective altitude gain.

JERRY RORERTSON

SUNDAY SOARING. *The last cup of coffee before a flight.*

TRAILING. *With one wing off, it can be readily seen how the fuselage and wings fit on a standard sailplane trailer.*

Execution was merciful. Lift changed into zero sink, then abruptly into 500 fpm down. Instantly, I made a survey of the terrain and saw a road branching into a Y with poles and wires along the upper left branch. By now there were only 800 feet of height left; we were sinking at a rate which would use that up in 95 seconds and flying just above stall speed—no time to be precise and methodical. In half a turn, I made the landing decision, then a diving 180 degree turn to gain reserve speed and line up with the intended road. Even with the dive we managed to get no more than 57 miles per hour indicated air speed. Forty feet above ground, we were lined up with the road, heading right into the wind and glare of a late afternoon sun. Visibility was poor because the canopy was dusted from wiping off breath condensation with my sleeve while at 11,000 feet. Then, two hundred feet ahead, from out of nowhere, appeared the enormous towers of a previously unobserved high tension line which had been camouflaged at altitude by the rough terrain and growth. I made an instant dive to pass under it, and we struck something—a powerline!

The heavy wire parted as it hit *Cirro-Q* directly on the nose, but the break was out left of the aircraft somewhere; the line was secure at one end and being drawn over the left wing, over the canopy and right wing. It was as if the whole sailplane were taking a drawn-out blow from a titanic, metal whip and there was a terrible whizzing sound as the wire cut deeply into the canopy at fifty miles an hour, one inch away from my skull. Control was unaffected in the next two hundred feet as we got down to eight feet above ground, when the free end of the wire shot over the left wing and canopy, then snagged the right wing. We were pulled up short, made a violent 120 degree aerial cartwheel and stopped, like an escaping boy caught by the wrist at a dead run and pulled off his feet by his own momentum. The nose fell to the ground and struck with a crunching bang. After a long flight the sudden absence of air noise bewilders; I heard only the loud ticking of my barograph and the sounds of a bitter wind which until now had helped me toward my goal. A 3/16 inch copper wire, ominous and malevolent, was wrapped about the right wing so tightly that the aileron was almost cut in half. Ten years of flying without accidents, over twelve hundred hours in aircraft doing no damage more serious than a scrubbed wingtip had just come to an end. I had busted one.

A quick survey indicated no personal injury, and nothing very wrong in the cockpit. After all the excitement, I did not reflect that if the powerline were alive, I would now be subjected to the most extraordinary encouragement to get out in a hurry, so I tried calling Bob Moore two or three times on the radio, then gave it up, wanting to get out before the crowd gathered. Gingerly, I stepped out; then came a horde of spectators and the police. We had crashed less than a mile from Boot Hill.

In Tombstone the people were magnificent. With help from the police, Bob found me in an hour. One man even drove into town and brought out some hot coffee which was more than welcome in the icy wind. By dark, we had my lovely, wounded bird again on its trailer. We were 176 miles from takeoff, only 32 miles from the goal, Silver C distance; after a first crackup with heavy damage to my sailplane, and still no closer to the easy Diamond— the Goal.

CHAPTER 12

Mountain Soaring at Bishop

Within forty-four hours after the crash at Tombstone, a survey of the damage had been made at Phoenix Airport. The right wing had been cut and heavily strained by the wire; there was buckling and other evidence of strain at the drag-spar bulkhead in the fuselage; the nose cone and a good bit of the forward underside of the fuselage were caved in. A mechanic, trained on 1-23 wings at Schweizer Aircraft, recommended taking *Cirro-Q* back to the factory where people had current experience working on the wings; and more important, where the wings could be put into jigs to see if there was hidden spar damage or bending. A few days later, Bob Moore and I started the long trip back to Elmira with *Cirro-Q* in tow. We averaged a thousand miles each twenty-four hours and got to Elmira two and a half days after leaving my house.

Next afternoon, we got the bad news that it would take at least three weeks to repair the sailplane.

Ruth Petry, former National Feminine Soaring Champion, who had recently moved to Phoenix, had her LK stored in the hangar on Harris Hill. The ship had no trailer, and it occurred to me that here was a chance to improve soaring fortunes in Arizona. I called her up, asked if she wanted her sailplane brought out, and she met the opportunity with great enthusiasm. Bob Moore and I spent a day and a half bringing the wings and fuselage of her ship down to the factory from Harris Hill and modifying *Cirro-Q's* trailer to accommodate a strange aircraft, then started the long drive home.

It was early June when we went back to Elmira the second time. I was accompanied by my sons John and Gregory who took care of Beebo. When the trip was finished, I had trailed over 10,000 miles as a result of the crash.

The next month, Ruth Petry crewed for me in a Fourth of July weekend contest which the Austin Soaring Club held at Georgetown, Texas. Our plan was to stop in Odessa on the way home and make a goal flight from Odessa to Liberal, Kansas, about 370 miles; good for a National record and two Diamonds. On the morning we left Georgetown, the sky was overcast and there was light rain, but that afternoon the sky took on the heart-breaking look of west Texas. There were powerful cumulus clouds from horizon to horizon; the sun appeared to be standing still and there was an illusion that we were in the sailpilot's heaven where a man could soar forever from cloudbase to cloudbase and the day never had to come to an end.

With high hopes, we drove toward Odessa, talking of great events and figures in the soaring world. Only two things disturbed me a little. The clouds were perfect, but the wind was not in the usual southerly direction. Why?

99

Then, fifty miles out of Odessa, the clouds vanished in mid-afternoon. Something was wrong with the weather.

At the Midland-Odessa Airport that night, I called Al Parker who agreed to tow on the following day. Then came a thorough briefing in the weather office. A gigantic front had invaded west Texas from Canada. It swung in a vast arc around Odessa, not two hundred miles away, and would certainly end a flight when a pilot came up against it. The wind shifted near the front and its flow was confused and erratic throughout the frontal region.

Cirro-Q never got off the trailer at Odessa that year. We headed home.

Jerry Robertson came with me again as crewchief during the National Soaring Contest, which in 1958 was going to be at Bishop, California. We planned to leave on Saturday before the contest and finally pulled out of my driveway at two o'clock, Sunday morning. By five, we were in Prescott and saw Bob Sparling leave in Dave Johnson's Super Cub for the contest. We drove past the Seligman Ridge, Hoover Dam, and Las Vegas; then down into the sun-blaze, heat-wave-trembling, barbaric splendor of Death Valley where the road goes far below sea level and fingernails feel like they are catching on fire; up over the middle range, down into the second valley, hoping the engine of the car will keep going and thinking maybe we had been well advised after all when they said not to pass this way in July, even with a big can of ice water along; then up over the second range with the pink rocks and late afternoon shadows; and at the summit you see across the Owens Valley for the first time—in the distance is the cool, gray-granite, jagged skyline of the Sierra Nevada with snowfields and the towering mass of Mount Whitney. Then down the mountain, across the last of the desert, and into Lone Pine where suddenly you find an icy mountain stream, grass meadows and poplar trees. Then, with evening gathering you go up the Owens Valley toward Bishop and on either side, over the Sierra and over the White Mountains, there are great piles of towering cumuli with bases over seventeen thousand feet high, and you know in the bones that glory is ahead and you will have a couple Diamonds in your hat before you return home.

We came into Bishop just before dark. Graham Thomson and the RJ-5 were already there, so was Dick Schreder and his new HP-8, and Hal Hutchinson with his beautiful little Prue 215. On Monday we got settled into the motel, registered for the contest, rigged the sailplane and had a miserable 15 minute test flight. The radios did not work, and I found no lift. One aircraft got up to 23,000 feet that day, and altitudes of 17,000 to 20,000 were common. There was the inevitable talk of mountain flying. I had never done any; few there had. Hal Hutchinson got within 300 feet of the rocks. "It's a little hard to judge the distance," he said. Bill Ivans was quoted as saying that fifty feet away the lift was about right. That evening we caught up on all the news of old soaring friends. Bob Schnelker had not been able to make it to the Contest.

On the first day, the task was a goal and return flight to Lone Pine, 56 miles out, for a total distance of 112 miles. Final preparations were hectic, and I took off with no lunch and no food; always an uncomfortable way to fly. Emergency gear, however, was very complete. I had the required oxygen equipment, flares, and emergency water, as well as a regulation canteen for drinking in flight. There was also an Air Force book on survival, a tiedown kit, signalling mirror, and infantryman's compass.

Release was 2500 feet above the Bishop Field a little east from the village of Laws over an alluvial fan at the base of the White Mountains. There is generally sink over the Owens Valley and it is necessary to get up over the mountain slope to gain lift. One of the problems was to estimate when to leave the mountain if lift was not encountered fairly soon after release. Glide angle calculations meant little when having to fly three miles through air which was sinking at an unknown rate in order to make it back to the field for another try.

Unlike straight thermal soaring, mountain flying is a combination of ridge and thermal work. You do not go up straight, but keep working in toward the side of the hill. On the first contest day, my rabbit foot was in hand. There was a good lift right off tow and before long we got up over the ridge east of Bishop, more than 11,000 feet high. The oxygen mask was put on, and we headed south toward Lone Pine. For some time the going was very good, and I only stopped to circle occasionally, flying most of the time at 60 miles an hour above the ridge, going straight toward the goal. Half way there, I passed the TG-3 being flown by Bill Ordway.

East of the turn point, I left the mountain, 10,500 feet high, about mountaintop altitude, without waiting to gain extra height for my dash over the Valley. Heavy sink was everywhere, and I made the turn over Lone Pine Airport, then ran for the mountain. Halfway back, I passed through some weak lift and ignored it. This was a race; why play with 150 fpm lift when only two miles away there is 400 to 800 foot lift? The sun was now in the west at midafternoon; it seemed impossible that there would be any trouble finding lift over the mountain, with the heavy rays beating directly on the rocks.

We got over the slope two thirds of the way from the base to ridgecrest and started sinking 400 feet a minute. In desperation I got in closer and closer to the rocks; I picked areas where the sunlight was strongest and where the wind seemed to *have* to go up. A steep valley was shielded on three sides from wind and almost luminous in the blaze of sunlight, a textbook thermal breeder if ever

STARTING LINE. *Slender wings of sailplanes form a tightly woven pattern as they work toward the head of the line in a National Soaring Contest.*

WING ROOTS AND CANOPY *have been sealed with masking tape to reduce aerodynamic drag. It is extremely hot in the cockpit until the aircraft begins to move.*

one existed. Things quickly changed. My rate of sink went from 500 to 750 feet a minute.

One mile west of Owenyo on the far side of high tension lines, there was a beautiful dry lake. I landed on it, then had quite some trouble calling contest headquarters. In two hours Jerry arrived. Only four people completed the task and next morning I found myself in sixth place out of thirty-two competing aircraft.

The second day they called for a triangular task, 30 miles north to Benton Station, then 57 miles south to Aberdeen, then back to Bishop. The whole flight could be made over the ridge of the White Mountains except for two dashes out over the valley to make the turn points. For me, everything went fine to start with. I found a good thermal after release and climbed rapidly to mountaintop. There was fast flying north to Benton Station with only three stops to circle for lift up to cloudbase. This was flying for the gods: a day any soaring pilot could dream about. My altitude varied from ten thousand to sixteen thousand feet; there was a chill in the brilliant crystal air, and camphor smell from the oxygen mask; there was quiet air noise and the heavy pull of breathing. From time to time I would be working in cloudshadow with another bright sailplane. We flew over White Mountain Peak, brown as cocoa, a spire with an incongruous road leading up to the summit over fourteen thousand feet high. A truck was parked beside a tiny wooden shack at the top, and the mountain fell away so steeply that it was not six miles to the valley floor, ten thousand feet below. The Owens Valley was in brilliant sunshine and on the far side was huge Mono Lake, then the steep pitch of the Sierra with many peaks over thirteen thousand feet, and tiny lakes in the high country which made it like an undiscovered place on the moon; and far above the high peaks were gigantic towers of cumulus. Eastward there was Fish Lake

Valley, again in brilliant sunshine; then the Silver Peak Mountains, then another valley, and mountains, and still another valley and mountains, each range becoming a fainter blue in the distance. Over the White Mountain ridge, towering cumuli were evenly spaced and up toward Benton Station the ridge flattened out; I flew over grassy mountain meadows and snowfields.

After making both turn points, at last we came around the slope of Black Mountain and saw the airport at Bishop. It seemed to be down at a 45 degree angle! There were only ten miles to go and over 4000 feet to play with so I pushed *Cirro-Q* up to 110 miles per hour. Now came a series of bumps so violent I was afraid of a skull fracture, and we slowed down to 90, then tried it fast again. More blows on the head. Maybe 90 is all right after all? We came in at 90, passing over the finish line 1200 feet high before making a pattern and landing.

Fifteen sailplanes completed the task that day, and I was one of the slowest, at four hours even. I had been on oxygen most of the time aloft, but still seemed to be taken with hypoxia. My fingernails were not blue, and I still had enough coordination that landing had not been difficult, but alertness and memory were gone as they are in a drunken man just before sleep. I could not remember which wingtip had the skid on it and which one had been left unguarded after being lost in the crash at Tombstone. Jerry ran up to grab the tip and ask if anything were wrong. I was ready for a rest.

The third day saw the most difficult task ever assigned at a U. S. National Soaring Contest: a goal-and return-flight to El Mirage and back. Total distance was 390 miles; the World Goal-and-Return record at that time was 320 miles. Dick Schreder and Harold Jensen completed the task but missed the record by landing too far away from release point, having been towed over the lower

White Mountain slopes, three miles from Bishop Airport where they landed.

I got a late start and missed getting away on first tow, an unlucky break which hurt badly at the end of the flight. I had announced my Goal as El Mirage Field, the turn-point which was far enough away to be good for a Goal Diamond. The prodigious nature of the conditions that day can be judged from the fact that I made 90 miles in the first two hours against a mild headwind, even counting the tow and initial climb to 14,000 feet. Most of the flying was straight away under a cloudstreet, with an occasional pause to circle for height if the lift ran over 1,000 feet per minute. This went on until I was at the south end of the White Mountains, 70 miles out. At this point, east of Owens Lake, I had to decide whether to continue over the low mountains ahead, or transfer to the southern end of the Sierra. I chose the Sierra, and it led to a most interesting flight. Eighty miles out, I left my last cloud at 14,500 feet. We ran south of Owens Lake approaching the Sierra in heavy sink. Ninety miles out, we were over the ridge with little height to spare and no clouds ahead for forty miles.

After a few minutes the reserve height was lost, and we began the tricky procedure of riding the ridge a few feet over the rocks. This worked very well over a descending ridge, but when the ridgecrest went back up, we could not hold onto it and had to slip over to the side. At one point, we were down a thousand feet below the crest, and I assumed the flight was almost over when I found weak lift over a brutally sharp ridge that plunged from skyline to valley floor at an angle of 50 degrees. It was one of a series of granite knife edges between steep gorges, like ribs holding up the spine of the mountain. If you were to crash on an Elmira-style ridge, it would be an easy walk to the telephone; on the White Mountains, it would be a job of days to get the wreckage out. On this ridge, if you caught a wingtip you would fall hundreds of feet before hitting the second time. A hunter might find you in deer season. Yet here we were, a few miles an hour above stall speed, painfully climbing the ridge fifty or a hundred feet at a circle; so close at the inner part of the turn that I had to bank the wings to parallel the upward thrust of the rock; so close that mechanical trouble seemed to develop in the chest, intestines, and belly. Any climbers on the mountain would have found it majestic to watch. At last, I got a few hundred feet over the summit and repeated the process, going down once only two hundred feet below skyline, once thirteen hundred feet, then six hundred. After forty miles of this, we left the mountains and went out over the desert where cumulus clouds lifted us to good altitude again.

We flew past Inyokern where Jerry was going to wait for me, then past Searles, Johannesburg, and Atolia; finally past Boron where I knew we could make the turn at El Mirage and get the first Diamond. Since our altitude was still good, the dream of getting back to Inyokern took shape. A storm had been moving north for some time and had passed the turnpoint. Fifteen miles north of El Mirage, we reached the storm and left a good thermal at 11,000 feet, then plunged under solid overcast into steady sink. We flew over the turn and made a hopeful dash back toward the sunlight and lift again, throwing away the Goal Diamond—across a dry lake, over the Shadow Mountains, and finally into sunlight over a little ranch ten miles of the way back. Ahead, up high, were cumulus clouds, but now it was five o'clock in the afternoon, too late to get back up again, and only 800 feet of altitude remained. Only ten miles flown on the return. I went back two miles to a broad side road we had passed over and landed without spoilers.

Five and a half hours we had been aloft, 195 miles against the wind, 203 total. Just eight airline miles away, across the Shadow Mountains, were friends, food, and a telephone. At one point in the flight, the Goal Diamond had waited for me, a tiny three thousand feet away, straight down. But now it was a two and a half mile walk to a ranch where some wonderful people gave me dinner, drove me 13 miles by road to the nearest telephone and waited up until I made contact with Jerry Robertson at one o'clock in the morning, after which they helped us de-rig *Cirro-Q*. We left there at 2:00 A. M. and got into Bishop at 8 o'clock. Pilots' meeting was at 9:30. I had slept on the way home and flew next day, the kind of thing you can only do with a first-rate crew chief.

Two days later was the first open day in which pilots could fly anywhere they chose in order to test their skill in the use of terrain and available weather conditions. The contest meteorologist held out promise of long flights being possible in the direction of Salt Lake City. I declared a goal near Wendover Air Force Base, 325 miles out and took off at 11:30. There seemed an excellent chance of getting one of the things I had come to Bishop for: two Diamonds on one flight.

At first, the going was very slow. It was even difficult getting to mountaintop. I had no radio contact with Jerry, but could raise contest headquarters and told them I was leaving after three quarters of an hour, even though I was not yet above the White Mountain ridge. Ruth Petry came with Jerry that day. At walking pace, we flew northward; then finally, an hour and a quarter out, we were ten feet above a saddle in the ridge, approaching it in sink at 45 miles an hour. Not quite enough altitude. In a fury I turned around and spent another fifteen minutes working slow lift on the side of a spire. We got two hundred feet higher and made another pass at the saddle. This time we only had five feet of clearance, but 70 miles an hour in speed. I zoomed over, ten feet above ground, and we immediately

TOM HENDERSON

CONTEST SOARING *at Bishop, California. An LK is about to get airborne on tow.*

TOM HENDERSON

CHAMPIONS. *Dick Schreder on aero-tow in his new HP-8 sailplane. He won the Twenty-fifth National Soaring Contest at Bishop.*

sank below crest on the east side of the White Mountains where clouds looked stronger. It was a good guess. Not long afterward we left Boundary Peak at 15,500 feet and headed toward Coaldale, the first real Nevada landmark.

Came the violent sink, over 1,000 feet a minute at any speed. I put the nose down until we were going 100 miles an hour and waited. More sink. It looked as if we would not even make it to Coaldale and would have to land on the dry lake short of the airport, an effective glide angle of only 10 to 1 from above the high mountain. Then 1,500 feet above ground, I got lift and slowly worked back to safe altitude. This climb took us another 25 miles along course at the end of which came another violent sinker which pulled us down less than 1,400 feet above ground, and I realized there was no hope of reaching Tonopah. Then the miraculous blessing of lift again!

By this time things had changed; the lift was not fast or violent, but slowly we circled up and up until the altimeter read 17,100 feet, the highest I had ever been in a sailplane. Over the radio I heard some less fortunate pilot inform his crew that he was going down at Tonopah. When you are high aloft, such a message gives a feeling of both pity and superiority.

When I was down low, short of Tonopah, I was only 70 miles out on course. Now, at high altitude and with relatively high speed, we passed the Tonopah Airport, eight miles east of the town; then came up to the Hot Creek range of mountains, and turned somewhat left at Warm Springs, 130 miles out. At this point the course turns from east to northeast, and we got much more help from the southerly component in the wind. I flew across Hot Creek Valley from 11,000 to 16,000 feet high, slowly getting numb with cold as we moved rapidly along our course.

The clouds ended 160 miles out and there were none ahead for 40 miles. The first ten miles in clear sky produced no embarassing sink and even some lift; but then it came: 1,000 fpm down. Again the long race at 100 miles per hour, past the Pancake Range, turning away from the road and out over a gigantic dry lake in Railroad Valley, plunging toward the slopes of the Grant Range which directly faced the westering sun. We arrived a scant 600 feet above the valley floor, near a ranch, and found zero sink. After prolonging the flight several minutes, we were down another 50 feet. As I turned downwind preparing to leave the slope and land at the ranch, I encountered a bubble of lift. We were so close to the mountain I had to turn left at first in order to stay clear of the rocks. For a time, every circle netted twenty or thirty feet gain in height. Look out there now, let's not pull another Tombstone! But there were good landing places all over the area and in 20 minutes we got back up to ridgetop height and worked slowly northward toward Currant. A break in the ridge cost us 200 feet, but it was quickly regained, and we were sure of getting as far as Currant. Beyond that village, the terrain was very rough, but I was working lift which I suddenly realized was a thermal, not just ridge flow, and we climbed back up to 13,600 feet, 8,000 above our low point on the Grant Range, as we blew (drifted while circling) slowly northward.

If I can just stay high like this when the air dies, I thought, we should be able to make a 40 to 1 glide with this tailwind. There isn't much daylight anymore, but we are already 210 miles out! Again the Distance Diamond seemed vaguely possible.

One last cloud was worked; then came another crashing sinker—1,000 fpm down all over again. Ten miles southwest of Ely, the terrain is 7,000 feet high. I tried once more to get in against a mountain, but three saves must have been my quota for that day. There was no lift. I made a short retreat and landed ten miles southwest of town on a broad airstrip beside the main road. We had been aloft seven hours and forty-two minutes and had flown 218 airline miles from Bishop. Helen Thomson drove up and stopped to say hello; Anna Saudek and Connie Ripley came by, crewing for Hal Hutchinson. Only 20 minutes after I was down, even before I had time to secure the aircraft, Ruth Petry and Jerry Robertson drove up. By road they had come 250 miles from Bishop. We were de-rigged shortly after sundown, and ate with a gang of soaring pilots in Ely, Nevada.

The final day was open; another chance to get Diamonds. Getting to mountaintop was difficult in the extreme, but at last we got over Boundary Peak, the usual 15,000 feet high, with the oxygen mask on. From north through east there was now a broad open area with no cloud, but beyond there, good cumulus began again, and I heard on my radio that conditions were fantastically strong at Tonopah. We plunged into the open area, found the expected 1,000 feet a minute sink and raced for the distant, promising cloud.

It was dead when we arrived. So was the next one, and the next and the next. I sneaked through a notch in the Silver Peak Mountains and arrived over a dry lake with 150 feet to spare—found patchy bubbles of lift and went down.

The landing was only fifty-five miles away from Bishop, south of Blair Junction a little beyond Coaldale. Eastward, over Tonopah, a gigantic thunderstorm was developing, and I watched it come toward me while I waited for Jerry who had been advised of my position by Dick Schreder who flew over and answered my radio call. Schreder flew on and landed miles away from help that afternoon, but his flight was long enough to hold onto the first place he had attained mid-way through the contest, and he landed his new HP-8 as the National Champion. The

HP-8 was the second very high-performance aircraft he had designed and built in a year and half—a job that would take most builders ten years. After the first day, he flew with grandeur. Never has a victory been more nobly won.

When Jerry arrived, we de-rigged *Cirro-Q* with frantic speed and had it safely on the trailer just as the storm was breaking. On our way home that afternoon, from the saddle north of Boundary Peak, we saw a lovely rainbow in the east.

The contest was over. We ended in 11th place. No Diamonds at Bishop.

CHAPTER 13

Another Diamond Try

Saturday, September sixth, was a day to get the easy Dia-
mond. Marcel Godinat and his wife Bertha were with me
in Prescott as crew, and Bob and Dottie Moore flew in at
10:00 o'clock for the tow.

After one letdown, we took a second tow shortly after
noon. I released in good lift at 2000 feet, a little south of the
field, and soon climbed up beyond 10,000 feet. A short
glide put us in fresh lift, and we soared to cloudbase at
12,600 feet. Another short glide at 90 miles per hour and
another climb, this time in even stronger lift, almost 1000
feet per minute average. Cruising speed picked up. Over
the summit of Mingus Mountain, I looked ahead and saw
a big dead area, or at least an open area for 15 miles, but
just short of Sedona excellent cloud cover picked up again.
This is a classical situation. If you aim at a good looking

TAKEOFF. *Wingtip runner. A split second ago; Ken Bawden released the wingtip of his TG-3 which will soon be airborne.*

LANDING. *Cirro-Q comes in at Prescott Airport under a magnificent soaring sky. Few cross-country landings are made at airports.*

cloud, it will be dead when you arrive—the trick is to discover a tiny one which is growing. Leaving the mountain at 12,600, I went down to 8000 under the distant cloud. It worked. Good lift, but only up to 9500. Now on to that cloudstreet up ahead. Thirty-five miles had been covered the first hour; it looked like a good 60 in the second. I wanted to make the goal in four hours if possible.

Here we are under the cloudstreet, black and beautiful up at the base; 500 fpm in the first thermal we hit. What's this? Zero sink? Up there a little farther. 500 fpm down? Ah, lift at last; feels strong. Variometer? 50 fpm. Maybe we're too close to that rain which is closing in from the east.

Slowly I made a retreat to get farther from the encroaching rain. Under each cloud I could gain only 200 feet, then lost 500 getting to the next one. Above the Mogollon Rim, I was on course east of Sedona; then down at rim top height, then we sank off the crest. There was a desperate search for lift under cloud southwest of town, then a dive for the airport. Lift came 200 feet above the strip. Again zero sink, lift, sink, zero sink. One hour and forty minutes after takeoff, we were down only 40 miles away from takeoff point. Another try for the easy Diamond; another failure.

After five weeks, I knew the season was over and there would be no more Diamond hunting until next year. One brilliant, blue October Saturday, I drove up to Prescott with two of my boys to get *Cirro-Q*. Summer was gone and there was a sadness about leaving the airport. I thought of the late afternoon a few weeks before when I had gone down three miles away from the field after soaring two hours above twelve thousand feet under solid overcast. The rain had come and passed several times that afternoon. Bob Moore spotted me from the Super Cub while I was walking to a telephone, then landed on the road and taxied with me back to the slope near where *Cirro-Q* had stopped. We dragged the sailplane up to the top of a little hill, connected the towrope, got in and began a tow, heading uneasily toward high tension wires. It took forever to get airborne, and just as I began to think of releasing, he zoomed over the powerline with reserve speed, and the danger was immediately replaced by a feeling of peace under a dark sky which was open in the west so the sun came through near the airport and made a rainbow which arched over a little herd of running antelope. There had been another time when he could not get me over 800 feet above the airport, and when I finally released we sank a hundred feet, then got a lift which took us to 1600; we sank again clear down to 360 feet, and I thought everything was over for the day—then came slow lift, and we gained altitude and finally made over 15,400 feet at cloudbase, a Golden Altitude gain and we flew sixty miles over forest out to Camp Wood and back, then to Jerome and Clemenceau, returning at a hundred miles an hour after a wonderful day.

It was over now, and Georgetown was over, and Bishop was over, and that year we had done no flying at Odessa. The afernoon was warm—a blue-sky, football day in autumn, and I knew there would be no Diamonds until next year.

CHAPTER 14

Across the Continental Divide

The Fourth of July weekend in 1959 showed promising weather and at dawn on July third, we left my place in Scottsdale — Beebo, John, Camille, *Cirro-Q* and I. Ruth Petry was to follow in my Piper at a more civilized hour to make the tows and crew.

By 9:00 o'clock we were all together at the end of runway 21 in Prescott. Breakfast had been eaten and prospects looked excellent. Convection was outstanding. A good wind from west-southwest would have made an ideal day for distance flying, but I thought the start would be too late, and the Prescott forecast was for an identical day on the fourth. In two hours the ship was washed, rigged, and loaded. Sandwiches were taken on, the camera checked, barograph sealed and turned on—all the details necessary to a Diamond Goal flight around a triangle. My turn

118

points were to be Seligman and the San Francisco Peaks. Takeoff was at 11:30.

After a short tow and a good notch on the barogram, we climbed rapidly and headed out on course. I had made a mistake on the radio installation and could transmit but not receive. It seemed unimportant. There was a good deal of 800 and even 1000 fpm lift and beautiful cumulus in all quadrants to the horizon.

The first 35 miles went very fast even against a cross-headwind. Then lift weakened for quite some time and the going into the strong wind got very slow. A new powerful thermal east of Seligman let us run for the turn which we made in one hour and forty-five minutes. 57 miles. Now a downwind run of 72 miles to the San Francisco Peaks. We should be home by five o'clock no matter what happens. One Diamond.

At first, we were very low after making the turn, then came good lift and fast cruising. In another hour, we were far past Williams, almost on the approaches to the majestic San Francisco Peaks. Momentarily the clouds got weak, and we played in bubbly air. I turned back toward the weak lift we had flown through—nothing. Two clouds were tried. More sink. We passed an 800 foot butte and sank beneath its crest. Then came more of the bubbles, that maddening sensation of flying in ginger ale and working every gust for all it is worth, but finding yourself a little lower after every circle. By now we were less than 500 feet above ground and over a suitable landing field. Being this low in strong wind made flying very difficult. On the down-wind side of each turn, I had to put the nose far down to maintain safe airspeed; on every upwind side of the turn, there was a strong illusion that lift had been found. At last I was headed upwind at 175 feet and seemed to be climbing again. There were only a few seconds to decide whether or not to make one more circle. A tall hill on my left greatly confused the airflow. I pulled on full spoiler and let down at an extreme angle to hit the field, sailed over a few grazing cows and landed. A rustic little cabin stood a hundred yards away, and pine timber surrounded the field. Time: 2:30 P.M. Overhead the towering cumuli drifted rapidly eastward, passing cloudshadows over the San Francisco Peaks, and the hole that had brought me down filled. It was a magnificent soaring sky, and I had to watch it from the ground. There was no one at the cabin, and I walked an hour and a half before getting a ride to a telephone.

At nine o'clock that night Ruth Petry, the children, and I got back together, and it was almost midnight before we had *Cirro-Q* on the trailer. I napped in the back of the station wagon as Ruth drove to Prescott where we arrived at three in the morning. Ruth Petry finally stopped beside a hangar at the Prescott Airport. Two bedrolls were pulled out, and I went to sleep on the dusty trailer while the children and Ruth slept in the Ford. At 6:00 o'clock we were awakened by the crashing din of an outdoor telephone bell on the hangar. It was time to get to work. My ship was completely dusted from the retrieve and needed a bath. After this was done we checked the weather hopefully. "Sort of an unknown quality today," the meteorologist said. No one had much to say at breakfast. I was tired. A limited goal was set: Santa Fe, New Mexico, 370 miles away. If I got anywhere near, it would be over the 500 kilometer Diamond Distance requirement (311 miles).

We were airborne again at 11:30. Convection was very powerful, so strong I had to dive over 100 miles an hour to notch the barogram. Only twenty seconds were necessary to get back into the lift, and we circled up in the first climb of the day passing over Marcel Godinat, Bertha, Mrs. Vest, Bob Sparling, and my crew, all of whom had helped me get started. The wind was good, and we made the first progress drifting as we climbed to 11,000 feet. A second thermal carried us to cloudbase, and then we flew rapidly toward Mingus Mountain. Unlike my flight across the Continental Divide to Grants which I had made six weeks before, this one started fast, and we were over the Verde Valley in less than half an hour, climbing 500 feet a minute in rain under a dark, heavy cumulonimbus and watching the ghost town of Jerome growing smaller, far below. The cloud was a big one, and because of the shadow it cast, I knew that altitude would be precious on the far side. We made half the distance to Sedona without losing altitude, then began to sink steadily. Back in sunlight over the Sedona airstrip, came weak lift which we gratefully worked up to the top. The gigantic anvil of the cumulonimbus cloud was now blowing northeastward, and I knew that all my course would soon be under cloudshadow. We headed for the 7000 foot Mogollon Rim without quite enough altitude to mount it. A mile from the actual rim I recalled my only Prescott cross-country of 1958 when we had been over the rim and had sunk off, before making a dash for the Sedona airstrip. This time it looked as though I would never even get up on the shelf. Then came a merciful lift of 1200 feet, and I was over the high country, a thousand feet above Northern-Aire Lodge with its handsome golf course and pool.

My course was toward Mormon Lake in heavily forested country where it takes altitude to fly even though it is dotted with meadows, but there could be no thought of proceeding on course right now because the anvil of the cumulonimbus I had passed under near Jerome stretched half way to Winslow and had now begun to spread out laterally. Going toward Flagstaff in reduced sink, I had covered only a few miles when I was down to 800 feet. Then came a difficult, bumpy thermal. We drifted on course to fly it, prepared to abandon instantly if it turned phony, because we were drifting over solid pine

121

timber and away from the marginal landing place I had in sight; but in a few minutes we were climbing steadily at 200 feet a minute. This one had saved the flight—at least for the moment.

We got up over 10,000 feet, 3000 above terrain in this thermal, high enough to tiptoe slowly toward Flagstaff and the good cumulus clouds east of there, away from the deadly shadow. The next forty minutes we spent working slowly up a flight of cumulus steps—across the gay boats on Lake Mary, over the feverishly crowded highway from Flagstaff to Winslow; steadily upward in sunlight and little shadows until, something over two hours out, we were at 13,000 feet, east of the San Francisco Peaks. With a feeling of triumph and joy, we headed straight for Winslow. There was no lift on this first long cruise of the flight.

Winslow came on the horizon and then came abreast as we sank endlessly. By the time the airport was passed, we were down again only 3000 feet above ground. The whole area was now in the shadow of my old friend, the Cottonwood cumulonimbus. Just past the town, I came upon a pathetic, stringy thermal, like a starving horse, which I worked for ten minutes without gaining even a thousand feet. The only possible thing to do now was go along on course. A landing seemed inevitable within fifteen minutes. The few sick looking cumulus clouds ahead were well out of range. Then came a second weak thermal, but this one improved with time, and we got back up to marginal cruising altitude half way to Holbrook before it quit. We headed on course and found violent sink. Almost immediately, we were back down crawling again; then we hit a boomer which carried us to 14,000, and we happily waved goodbye to Holbrook. After all the recent anxiety we cruised only 60 miles per hour to save altitude. Finally, we ran beyond the Cottonwood cloud, but ahead there were two more which had spread out leaving a narrow corridor-like band of sunlight, in between shadows that covered hundreds of square miles.

We flew into the sunlight but found nothing. The red pellet of the Cosim variometer seemed glued in place in absolutely stable air. We sank exactly as fast as we were supposed to at 60 miles an hour; it was like December flying. I tried going under the edge of the shadow. No change. Finally, we came under a small cumulus in the shadow of high cloud. No change. Down past 12,000; 10,000; 8000, and 7000. I turned on the radio and put on my earphones.

"Zuñi radio, this is Schweizer 91899. This is Schweizer 91899, a sailplane, I am going down 20 miles east of Adamana. Going down 20 miles east of Adamana. Please give my position to my crew if they call you. They are following with a car and a trailer."

We turned left so the last thousand feet could be used to get near the railroad. Ahead there was a cattle tank, something that looked like a structure, and plenty of clear terrain for landing. At 6100 feet, 1100 feet over terrain, we hit a bump. I could hardly believe it. Then it was smooth again; then a series of bumps, one of which even raised the somnolent green pellet. We started a turn in reduced sink and from time to time the Memphis variometer needle would rise clear up to zero.

After sinking to 800 feet things got much better. We gained three hundred, very slowly, but solid gain. Then our lift ended, and we went down again by agonizing inches. Two miles northward, I saw a little dust devil go by. So near, and yet out of range!

Repeatedly the lift failed, and we worked north toward the dust devil area where it always again picked up. No gain, no loss in the next place we turned. How I wish this zero sink business could be what it sounds like, just going around like a coffee grinder, instead of having to work each gust with despairing precision to come out even at the end of every circle. We lost the three hundred feet and during that time drifted over higher ground, so we now flew just 700 feet above the lonely windswept mesa. Well, I gave it everything I had. 163 miles. It could be worse, but it's going to be a hell of a long walk to the road. The circling went on at 700 feet.

Then, from one second to the next, zero sink changed into 500 fpm lift. Three minutes later, 1500 feet higher, it steadily changed to 600 then into 800 fpm lift. At 12,000 feet it weakened, and we left; five minutes later came another one which carried almost to 14,000 feet. The whole area was under solid cloudshadow, and we slowly cruised eastward in greatly reduced sink. Losing only a thousand feet, we covered the next twenty miles without making a turn.

"Zuñi radio, Zuñi radio, this is Schweizer 91899, a sailplane. I am passing your station at 12,000 feet. Would you pass this information on to my crew if they call you?"

He said he would. I found out he had not received my transmission east of Adamana; I had been too low. This happy state was too good to last. We flew over Black Rock and the Zuñi Reservoir, and presently came up to Ramah with its long, slender lake. We had been aloft five hours and were within a few miles of the position we had been over at the five-hour mark on the flight to Grants. It was the same place trouble had started before and it started now again. Sink began to increase. Every cloud we got under seemed to have passed its prime; the good lift was always ten miles ahead. One thermal was worked for twelve minutes to gain a thousand feet which was lost in two and a half minutes. We still had almost 11,000 feet, but were sinking and coming to the Continental Divide where we had to cross the Zuñi Mountains with ridgetops all over 9000 feet high.

As we flew under a spent looking cloud over the plateau, I wondered if the flight would end in a narrow meadow, running between two ridges. No, maybe not yet. This cloud had lift. Only 50 to 75 feet a minute, but steady and without patches of sink to dodge as in the last two thermals. Below and just a little ahead, a fire sent out a long gray plume of smoke pointing right on course. I circled and drifted. In ten minutes the fire was well behind; in twenty minutes it seemed remote. We had passed lovely Bluewater Lake; Grants lay just ahead, far below. We had soared over the Continental Divide a second time.

My longest previous flight—265 miles—had ended in the eastern part of Grants. Now came a strong thermal under cloud—1000 feet a minute again. We went up to 12,000, then back to cloudbase. I talked with Grants radio, giving my position and altitude, and indicating that I was trying for Santa Fe.

My former landing place in the subdivision passed underneath, and we flew south of Mt. Taylor. Then a sudden change came in the air. Thermals got very close together, hardly five miles in between, and where above Grants there had been 1000 fpm lift with strong sink in between, now the lift was only 500 feet per minute. More significantly, the sink tapered off and became very moderate. The day was dying.

I changed my flight plan and radioed Grants. With stabilizing air, Santa Fe would now be nearly impossible to reach, and it would make a very difficult retrieve if I went down on the almost roadless desert between the two cities. We set course for Albuquerque and stayed close to the road. Most of the next 25 miles from south of Mt. Taylor to Correo, we spent circling and drifting on course. The short cruises between thermals grew shorter and the time climbing longer and slower with each lift. At Correo the railroad passes underneath Highway 66 and the highway turns east-northeast, straight toward Albuquerque, thirty miles away.

In great circle distance, I was 295 miles out, working the last thermal of the day; drifting steadily on course and hoping to get up to 11,000 feet one last time. We did not quite make it. At 10,700 the lift stopped. It became weak sink, and *Cirro-Q* and I headed for Albuquerque in the final glide through still air; the first time we had ever been aloft when thermals had quietly died.

Trying to fly without yaw, I began to measure the distances to Kirtland and West Mesa Airports and to make glide angle calculations. Getting to Kirtland Air Force Base in eastern Albuquerque looked just barely possible with no spare altitude. We flew along the road toward West Mesa Airport, slowly passing cars on the highway and arrived over the field with 1500 feet of height remaining. We were two miles west of the Rio Grande River on the western edge of Albuquerque. It was a few minutes before seven o'clock. We did a 180 degree turn to see the wind-sock, then made a wide circle around the airport, dropping the nose at the last moment for extra speed.

The wheel touched ground at exactly 7:00 o'clock after a flight of seven hours and thirty-two minutes, and the sound of the barograph ticking seemed very loud in the sudden absence of air noise.

We had flown 326 miles, 15 miles over the 500 kilometer Diamond Distance requirement. One sparkler for my Golden C Pin! Two men from a nearby subdivision helped me fill out the required papers and signed as witnesses to the landing, which they had seen from their swimming pool after I went over them on final approach.

In a remarkable job of crewing, Ruth Petry reached Albuquerque and found me before I had been down three hours. That night I saw only a single Roman Candle shot off in the distance on the bank of the Rio Grande River, but it was the happiest Fourth of July celebration in many a year despite my exhaustion. On the Fourth of July in both 1957 and 1958, I had flown failures for the want of only 500 feet of altitude. The Goddess of Luck had returned to me this day.

CHAPTER 15

The Great Climb

Although the forecast was for continued Pacific air during the first ten days of July, a few days later the monsoon came over the horizon and by the 11th it was in full sway with enormous cumulonimbus developments in all directions around Prescott, and wind from southeast. During the next weekend, I attempted four flights. We scarcely got over ten thousand feet, a mighty comedown from the glory of the week before when we had flown to Albuquerque.

Marcel's LO-150 was in the municipal hangar, and I put *Cirro-Q* in facing it. That week brought the first of of the violent summer storms and heavy damage at the airport, but luckily the wind hit the back of our hangar squarely and both sailplanes were protected. *Cirro-Q* was moved at the first opportunity into an enclosed hangar near the weather station.

By July 23rd there were completed plans to spend a long weekend in Prescott making a determined bid for the Diamond Altitude gain in which a sailpilot must gain 5,000 meters, 16,404 feet above the low point of his flight. Since Prescott is 5,000 feet high and there is difficulty getting started lower than 1,500 feet above terrain, a minimum altitude of about 23,000 feet would have to be made. I asked Jerry Robertson to crew and being unable, he introduced me to one of his mountaineering friends, Dick Hulme who did a superb job. Dick took all the gear, Camille, and Beebo in the Ford Ranch Wagon while I took John up with me in the Piper. The flight to Prescott was uneventful until we got over Mayer where we passed through a long area of 1,800 foot a minute lift, followed by such violent sink and turbulence that I reduced speed clear back to 80 miles per hour. It was a hopeful sign. We met at the airport in late afternoon, got a room at the Mission Motel, and eagerly awaited the events of the morrow.

Cirro-Q was already assembled in the hangar, and we only needed to wash the ship and get the equipment ready for flight. All this was accomplished by 11:00 A. M. Then I went in to see the mechanic who had agreed to tow that weekend, but he said he had become far too busy for any towing and would be "tied up" until Thanksgiving time. Great.

I went into the FAA office and asked if there were any commercial pilots with light airplane time in the area. Within twenty minutes they had one of their own people, a DC-3 pilot named John Woods, at the airport, and I was checking him out in my Piper. He got the feel of the airplane very quickly and after half a dozen landings dual, I let him go solo and went in to eat lunch. The day had

129

a very different look than it had worn only forty minutes earlier.

Dick Hulme and I got *Cirro-Q* up to runway 3, saddled up, and made the first tow at 12:45. I released at 1300 feet and made a dive to 1000 for a low notch on the barogram to minimize the disadvantage of the high field elevation. The notching procedure continued against my will to 900 feet where we hit rapid sink and went down at 500 feet a minute. I landed seven minutes after takeoff, before John Woods could even get down in the Piper. We quickly got ready for a second try. The barographs were never turned off; last minute instructions were given on wingtip running and towing; the canopy was resealed and at one o'clock *Cirro-Q* and I were off again behind a very good tow. This time release was made a little northeast of the field at 1700 feet and the dive was to 1400, 6400 feet above sea level. After 35 seconds at the low altitude, we got back into lift, which averaged 500 feet a minute, and climbed up to 12,000 without ever pausing.

From there, I tried to produce a spin, the emergency maneuver pilots can use if they became disoriented and want to lose altitude without gaining dangerous speed. I used every trick I knew attempting to spin in either direction, but finally gave up after pulling five G's on the sailplane in a spiral dive; 3700 pounds effective weight had been loaded on an airframe which weighs not much over 500 pounds while sitting empty on the ground. No emergency exits today.

Apparently the center of gravity was too far forward, with the radio and batteries for the electric turn-and-bank mounted in front of me. This was the first time I had a little German Friebe electric turn-and-bank mounted as a standby. The first minute I tried the instrument, I had such powerful vertigo it was almost impossible to hold out for sixty seconds. After a short rest, I tried it for 75 seconds, then three minutes, five minutes, and finally ten. By that time it was much easier, and I was able to relax with the instrument. Altitude was no problem; we had only once been down as low as 11,000 after the attempted spin. We were up toward Ashfork, well north of any airway, for the instrument practice; after an hour of intermittent work, I felt ready for the assault.

A week before, Marcel had been over 18,000 feet and was still gaining altitude outside of cloud by soaring up the brilliant side of a large cumulonimbus. He might have made Diamond Altitude had he not run out of oxygen. Now, there was a long mass of active cloud beginning south of Ashfork and running southeast.

The sun was shining powerfully on one side and my plan was to make the climb as Marcel had done. Only one difficulty stopped me: there was no lift anywhere along the supposedly active edge of the clouds. At one time we got up to 16,400 feet and headed for the edge, but were down to cloudbase and in sink when the critical position was reached. I was reporting to Dick Hulme by radio three times an hour, but there was little enough to report except that staying up was very easy.

We worked this area for an hour and three quarters without ever getting over 16,400—exactly 10,000 feet gained—6,404 feet short of the mark, almost two thousand meters. At last I gave up and headed toward Prescott once again. Today had produced some good results, and I felt optimistic that the climb could be made on Saturday or Sunday. We had been aloft exactly three hours when the big sink arrived. In four minutes I went down from 13,000 to 9000 feet. This was only 4000 above terrain; if it continued, we were much too far north to get back to the field. It had been caused by another mass of cloud, also oriented northwest-southeast. Early during the sink I turned in the direction of the sunny edge and nosed down until we indicated 90 miles an hour. Presently there was a violent bump which ended the crashing descent. The climb back toward safe cruising altitude began at 8800 feet in the roughest thermal of the day. Lift of 300 feet per minute gradually went up to 500. Above 14,000 it got smooth and went up over 800 feet a minute. . . .

Under conditions of reduced visibility the climb continued: 15,000, sixteen thousand, seventeen. 17,100 feet on a cross-country out of Bishop was the highest I had ever been in a sailplane. 18,700 was the State Altitude record. Might go for that one today. The smooth lift increased steadily; now it was 1500 feet a minute. I had planned on leaving the area now, but at 19,000 feet the golden bell of opportunity began to clang. The inside of my canopy was now completely iced up; lift on the Memphis variometer indicated almost 2000 feet a minute; sound effects from hail on the outside were increasing, but my speed ran a steady 45 to 55 miles per hour. The shallow-bank right turn continued.

I set the thermal-timer needle on the clock which now read 3:09. Climb until 3:15 and you will have it no matter what. Speed 51—needle, a little closer to center, that's it, ball O. K. Speed 47, a trace forward stick now, needle O. K. Altitude—21,300. Tap it, 21,700. Lift now pegged at over 2000 fpm. Needle a little more to right—left stick to bring up the ball—airspeed 55, trace back pressure. Time? Three minutes to go. Altitude 22,500. That's funny, should be higher. Lift—down to 1500 fpm, no there it goes again, up over 2000. Needle O. K. Ball, come on now, center up. That's better. Airspeed 48. Lift still over 2000. Altitude 22,500. More oxygen now, don't forget that. Three deep breaths, O. K. You should have the mask on up here, but don't try it now. 22,500 was that? Yes. Tap it. 22,500. Lift 1900 right now. Tap again hard. 22,500. Oh, I catch on. Either it's against the stop or frozen. No need to tap it again. Lucky. That last time felt like my fingertips were frozen. Legs not cold yet, even feet not too bad. Why are you shuddering all over? Tighten the belly. That helps. Airspeed 70. Needle way out. My God. Pay attention. Fly the sailplane. Oxygen now, quick. Ball in, needle coming back—easy on the back pressure—DON'T STALL. That's coming around. 58, a little more now—60. Needle, still O. K. There it is now—52. Time: two minutes to go. Very cold all over now. More oxygen. Quit shuddering. Lift still almost 2000, *seems like quite a while since it was down at* 1500.

Time: 3:14. *Five minutes since* 19,000. *Most of it over* 1500 *fpm. Hell, most of it over* 2000. *No. You haven't been watching it that close. But you only need* 23,000. 19 *plus four minutes gives* 23, *even at only* 1000 *fpm. It was never below* 1500 *fpm, right? Mostly* 1800 *or over* 2000. *OXYGEN now, QUICK. Needle O. K. Ball, not too bad. Airspeed* 56. *Altitude* 22,500. *Tap it.* 22,500. *It quit you idiot. Are you sure? Hell yes I'm sure. Need* 23,000. *Or is it* 25,000? *I wish to God I knew how high I am. Two and a half minutes since* 22,500, *right? Now over five minutes since* 19. *Quit shuddering. You aren't that scared. The ice? You can see the wings a little through the back edge of the canopy. Not too bad. Ship handles O. K. Turbulence now though. Will it get bad?*

O. K. We have enough. You win. Steer south . . .

South *you idiot, not northeast. OXYGEN. Course better now. That's it, now hold it. Needle center, airspeed* 55. *Very cold now. Shuddering uncontrollable. Hail noise heavy. Oxygen, more of it. Don't forget. Course* 210; *left needle. Hold it. Now center. Too far. Adjust again. Airspeed* 52. *O.K. God, are you drunk? Hold it on south, idiot, south. OXYGEN. Time* 3:18, *no* 3:19. *South. Needle center, ball center, airspeed* 54; *no lift anymore, sink beginning; now getting strong. Much lighter outside the canopy;*

no turbulence at all. No sound effects; no more hail, just quiet air noise. Oxygen again. Three deep ones. O. K. Better. Time 3:21. Try the canopy. No, you can't get your handkerchief out of the pocket under the seat belt. Use the sleeve—just don't scratch hell out of your canopy with the button. O. K. Try it.

That first view showed us close up underneath a mighty anvil. Ice an inch thick and two inches from top to bottom had formed over the leading edge of *Cirro-Q's* lovely wing. I wiped off another hole on the other side, then one at the top, and opened the airvent to get a blast of ice and freezing air. Vast, mountainous clouds were on all sides except for small openings. The descent had begun; we were losing a steady 400 feet per minute as we maneuvered in clear air, passing sometimes through narrow crevasses that seemed of rocklike solidness. The altimeter began to work again below 22,500. At 21,000 the freezing cold seemed to encompass everything, and I only felt a painful numbness.

The canopy gradually cleared as I wiped away at it, then stopped frosting over after each clearing. After some time the sky opened, and we came to an area where on one side I could even see a patch of horizon. We slipped through this cloud canyon and the whole western horizon came into view. A distant cumulonimbus mass hid the sun behind very active cells with boiling tops which were edged with luminous gold; some had great anvils at the summit and one or two were dropping heavy shafts of rain to the ground—a scene full of disturbing wonder and glory.

Inside the icy cockpit the glow of victory was becoming stronger than the cold. You did it! You did it!! You're a two Diamond man! *Cirro-Q*, you're a two Diamond ship! You have flown higher over Arizona than any sailplane.

Four hundred feet per minute down. At 15,000 feet the ice began to go, melting drop by drop at first and disappearing into the air behind, then getting soggy. At 12,000 feet it was coming off in chunks and making collision-like noises when it struck the tail feathers. We flew very high over Prescott, then once again later as we were getting ready to land. A final radio report was made.

The landing was at 4:00 on the aircraft clock and the glow of triumph was full in the breast and the warm air a merciful blessing to chilled legs and feet. The barographs were ticking their cheerful little message, and I could see part of one trace on the smokedrum through the windows of the Lange, but neither this one or the Peravia could be opened now. That had to wait for Bob Sparling who had sealed them.

We put *Cirro-Q* away for the night and took the yarn yaw indicator from the canopy and stuck it on the inside of the Ford's windshield for a battle trophy as we had done at Albuquerque. After dinner that night, we saw Bob Sparling. When unsealed, the barograms indicated a peak altitude of 26,083 feet; 19,683 feet gained—almost exactly 6000 meters.

CHAPTER 16

Record Soaring Camp at Odessa

*Through most of my days in soaring, I have had the won-*derful companionship of a German Shepherd named Beebo. Many is the night he slept by me on the ground beside the trailer, close to a bedroll. Other times, he has been with me in a motel during the last anxious hours before a long flight. He has been the first to greet me after landing and has come home on the long retrieves.

After much planning for a soaring trip to West Texas, at nine o'clock one evening we left for Odessa, a happy family. I was the pilot; Ruth Petry, crew chief; and Beebo was her right-hand man. Also along were *Cirro-Q* and my sons John and Gregory. I had packed the Ranch Wagon as carefully as my limited ability would permit and everything went fine until we had covered thirty miles, when I became too hungry and sleepy to drive. We stopped for a second dinner and coffee at Apache Junction, but the coffee was not strong enough. I gave up and let Ruth drive.

The back of the Ranch Wagon was crammed with suitcases, radios, canteens, a footlocker for general soaring gear, toolbox, parachute bag, and all kinds of other equipment. The only thing I was interested in at that hour was the bedroll with the air mattress underneath. Beebo had been trying it out and found it quite satisfactory, but when I shoved him over on the cardboard suitcase his morale collapsed. As the night wore on, we could hear his claws scratch the cardboard in a vain effort to hold on. It made a sound like fingernails being scraped against a blackboard, and every time a curve was rounded he slid off. I thought this was hilarious; he thought it was unspeakable and thought he was being treated in a manner unbecoming an old soaring dog. He began to look at the whole expedition with a cold eye of disapproval. For over a year he had regarded the Ranch Wagon as his personal property, and he thought it was bad enough to clutter up the back with all that junk, but having a woman along was inexcusable.

It is always difficult to sleep in a station wagon the first night out, but I finally dropped off. It was deep and peaceful until I had a terrible nightmare about getting crushed under an avalanche. I awoke, struggling, and found Beebo asleep on top of me. There was a sudden flailing of arms, and I expressed a profane opinion of dogs who crawled over and went to sleep on top of sleeping pilots. He went back to the suitcase, resentful but contrite, wearing an expression like a dog who has just had a stolen beef roast forcibly removed from his jaws. When I took over the driving again a little before dawn, he immediately asserted his rights. After all, *he* owned the back of the car; even *I* had never challenged his reign there. When Ruth tried to settle down for sleep on the bedroll, Beebo moved in with an authoritative growl. From the wheel I explained

137

to him that he would have to sleep on the little suitcase. He complied almost immediately, but moved over on the bed-roll again after I had the station wagon cruising along. It was finally settled between them that Ruth would get two thirds of the bedroll and Beebo one third. Under conditions of this uneasy truce, they both went to sleep.

We stopped for breakfast at Clint, Texas, southeast of El Paso on the Rio Grande River. After driving hard through the day, we arrived at Odessa a little after four in the afternoon. This was the fourth day of the 1959 Odessa Soaring Camp and the weather was said to have been disappointing so far. Dick Schreder had arrived that morning. Next day, we found out that Harland Ross, designer and builder of the RJ-5 and R-6, who the year before had flown his beautiful R-6 to three world speed records on three consecutive days, had a very different estimate of the weather. On the day we arrived, he had flown 365 miles and made a Diamond Altitude gain. This made him U. S. Diamond C number 14, a remarkable flight because there was no tail wind at all. We said hello to old soaring friends and got settled in the hotel by dark. At the hotel, we were told the news of Bob Schnelker's death on a flight out of Odessa two days before. He had previously won his Altitude and Goal Diamonds and had been over half way toward the Distance Diamond when his sailplane broke up in mid-air as the result of a mistake he had made in rigging. There was sorrow in reflecting that a pilot who had worked so hard for his Diamond and who had come so close, never got it, but instead found a gravestone.

Next day we were late getting started to work, but the weather also took its time. It was almost two o'clock in the afternoon when I was towed off behind Al Parker's mighty BT-13. This aircraft has been modified and it carries a 650 horsepower engine. Two minutes and twenty seconds after he advanced his throttle, I released at 1800 feet between Odessa and the airport. The barogram was notched and then we found nothing but sink. I made the first landing only ten minutes after takeoff even though a little circling had been done just outside the field pattern. At 2:15 we were off again behind Dave Johnson's Super-Cub; the barograph was on; my goal was Hereford, Texas, southwest of Amarillo, 195 miles away. Nothing more has to be said about the expectations of Texas weather when a pilot makes a serious try for a Diamond Goal flight starting after two o'clock in the afternoon.

Convection was powerful. We left Odessa at 8000 feet after a thermal which indicated our cruising speed should be 85 miles per hour between lifts. With the tail wind we started covering ground at 100 mph between thermals. It was going to be a race with the sun; we could only hope that lift would remain good until six o'clock.

For the first hour and a half, we had conditions which have made West Texas famous around the world as a paradise for cross-country soaring. We smoked by Andrews and Seminole, then passed Seagraves and went over the highway at Wellman. Ninety miles out, the town of Brownfield appeared on the right; we were getting uncomfortably low; the clouds were not building as they had, and for a little while we flew at maximum glide in search of a thermal. The day was no longer as strong as hoped for; even back at 7000 feet we had to slow down. The last thermal had been weak, but now sink was strong and thermals were widely separated. Very soon we were down low again. After the next climb we continued the flight at maximum glide angle, and my hope for success gradually tapered off. A town with the discouraging name of Sundown passed slowly by, to the left of course; then Levelland, Whitharral and Littlefield.

Still almost seventy miles to go and a painful decision to make; should we leave the good airport at Littlefield?

A disciplined sailpilot cannot throw away altitude while there is a possibility of evening thermals. Fifteen miles later, we got a thermal at 1200 feet over a dry, sandy river-bottom. This carried up over 2000 feet and made it easy for us to pass over Springlake, but the end was at hand. Nothing further came. Eight miles north of Springlake, *Cirro-Q* turned around, made a retreat over Running Water Creek and landed almost exactly on the border of Castro County in a good field half a mile from the road. The Goal Diamond requires a flight of 300 kilometers, 187 miles, to a specified airport or field which has been announced before takeoff. We were thirty-nine miles short.

It was my twenty-second attempt at the Diamond Goal, the "easy" Diamond, ranging back to 1956 when on one occasion I had flown 130 miles in the Baby Albatross on a day with no tail wind. A number of times the flights had been over 200 miles, but never to a goal. One of them ended in the crash at Tombstone, just 32 agonizing miles from my Goal; one found the Goal only three thousand feet away, straight down, but it was a contest day; there was altitude left at my Goal of El Mirage and a possibility of going on to get more contest points. Another flight took us east from Prescott over the border of New Mexico and the Continental Divide—the first such flight since Peter Riedel had done it back in 1939 in a Kranich—but I went down at Grants, 265 miles out. Six weeks later, there was the attempt at a goal flight from Prescott all the way to Taos, New Mexico, and the landing was a miserable 26 miles out.

Now the twenty-second failure had been flown. I walked up and down the country road for two hours listening to the buzz of insects and the occasional roaring swish of a car or truck running by as the sun got lower. Then Ruth came and by hurrying, we just managed getting de-

SOARING FLIGHT. *Harland C. Ross designed and built his R-6 sailplane. In 1958 he flew it to three World Speed Records on three consecutive days.*

A SCHWEIZER *1-23D on tow above Chemung Valley. Behind the sailplane is famous Harris Hill.*

rigged before it grew dark. Final inspections were made with a flashlight.

On the way home serious personality problems began to develop between Ruth Petry and Beebo. She was tired from the long drive to Odessa, and he was a little short tempered. Relations deteriorated, as they say in diplomatic circles. Ruth was aware of his smell and by imperceptible degrees had stopped calling him Beebo and started referring to him as B. O. She had never seen him at home, in his glory, sneaking up on the neighbor's collies—one step at a time, crouched low, with eyes narrowed to a slit and the hair standing up on his back, just like an O. S. S. man in the movies. Neither did she appreciate the great youthful enthusiasm with which he leaped about the back of the car to bark at dogs, boys, old ladies, young ladies, men on motorcycles and bicycles, and especially horses, cows and geese. Another thing which got on her nerves, aside from his ticks and halitosis, was what she called the "Beebo Shudder." When Beebo shakes, he develops enormous power. The movement runs like a wave from his head to the shoulders, belly, and hips. I have often wondered how the hip joints could stand so much violence without getting "thrown out." It is impressive and convulsive and while it goes on, he radiates a smog-like substance composed in varying quantities of dog-smell, hair, dust, and farts.

From where Beebo sat, he was doing his very best to be broad-minded. Good show type of thing—make the best of a bad situation, live and let live. For some reason he did not understand, the master wanted him to share *his* part of the car with *that woman,* and the master had filled the back of the car with all sorts of obstacles which made footwork very difficult at best when a fellow jumped around.

After stopping for dinner which we shared with Joe Emmons and Doc DeGinder, we were driving back toward

Odessa. Ruth had gone to sleep in the back, John was in the back, Gregory was asleep on the front seat, and Beebo was sitting up on the front seat beside me, intently watching the road.

Then it happened. A tremendous white-face cow lifted her head as we approached. The headlights flashed in her eyes, and she began to move across the ditch away from the road. Beebo took in the situation at a glance, made one great leap from the front seat clear to the back of the car, and at the same time let go a single bark which had all the concussive effect of a dynamite blast. Then he sat down and put on the satisfied grin of a man who knows he has done a hard job well. At least one cow really knew where she stood.

Unfortunately, and through no fault of his own, he had landed on Ruth Petry's head. She was probably dreaming about her work in Aviation Crash Injury Research and one can imagine her mental fantasy of an aircraft flying about, and how the thing which had just happened could easily have been misinterpreted as the impact of a crash.

Instantly she sprang up shouting: "Help, get the fire-engines!" In a minute she began to realize what had actually happened and started mumbling. I could not make out the words, but I suspect it was the most unprintable muttering of the year. She had no word of praise for the athletic ability of an old dog who could make it clear across the car in one leap from a sitting start; no suggestion of approval for the restraint Beebo had shown, because in all West Texas he had waited until he spotted *the* cow.

I realized a crisis was at hand. After stopping the car and trailer, I turned around and started to berate Beebo who was grinning like a politician. Ruth Petry was still enraged. Suddenly, it struck me as unbearably funny. It was a very dark night, and several times I averted my face and carefully studied the horizon while I shook with quiet laughter. I can only hope Ruth Petry mistook this for quiet sobs of frustrated anger—a strong man who did not want to show his weeping face to a girl.

By now she was completely awake and took over the driving. I thought it might help the situation if Beebo were put into a condition of semi-banishment. With this in mind, I put him down on the floor just ahead of the front seat on the right-hand side. He tried to escape two or three times until I sternly commanded him to stay. We started off and soon I fell asleep.

It seemed only a few minutes later when the car stopped again. Beebo was sitting up on the floor with a tremendous grin on his face.

"What happened?" I asked sleepily.

"Beebo threw up on the floor," she said furiously. "Remind me *never* to travel with a dog. UuaaGH!!!*?!" This last was a rare sound; even in huge colored letters it could not be adequately represented by print. It was a combination of horror, loathing, disgust, humiliation, and despair. It was as if for the first time in her life she realized all she had missed by not having a dog—and was grateful to the bottom of her soul.

We got home at 1:30 in the morning, dropped off *Cirro-Q* at the airport, and went on to the Lincoln Hotel. Next day, I attempted a Diamond triangle. The first eighty miles were into a sixteen-knot wind. Three times we were almost down. I made the first turn; then soon afterward the triangle was abandoned, and we tried to get home. After a long struggle, we landed short, only six miles from Ector County Airport—my twenty-third try for the Goal. De-rigging was accomplished in the half light of dusk and weather was checked at the main airport of Midland-Odessa. Nothing big tomorrow; it would be a rest day.

It turned out far better than expected. I could not resist the look of the clouds and went up to fly locally almost four hours. That night I checked the weather again and picked a Goal in the west because the forecast predicted a light easterly wind and heavy cumulonimbus buildups to the northeast all the way around to south, which would probably bring a sailplane down before the day was over. My Goal was tiny McCoy Field, 62 miles southeast of El Paso on the Rio Grande River. It was 213 miles along the road from Odessa's Ector County Airport, and 204 miles by great circle. The Post Office name of the hamlet there is *Esperanza*, the Spanish word for hope.

CHAPTER 17

Flight to Esperanza

Early next morning, I sent John down the hallway to knock on Ruth Petry's door and make certain she was up. He outdid himself and knocked on everybody's door. He did not realize there were some people there who were not in soaring and our popularity on the floor dropped sharply.

Out at the field nobody seemed to have much optimism.

"It doesn't look very good today, I think I'll take this one off." A general impression of the weather. It was August eighth.

"Oh, I didn't know you had your Altitude Diamond," said Pop Krohne to me, "You have the Distance too? Only the Goal left? There's nothing to it. Why don't you go to Hereford? That's where I got mine."

Harner Selvidge looked at the sky. "Anyway, if you don't get it in Texas, you can still try at home."

Cirro-Q was rigged and clean from the day before. We put in the gear, checked radios, got food aboard and made all preparations by 11:00. Overhead there was high cirrus in a very thin overcast; there was not a cumulus cloud to be seen. At 11:15 tiny cumuli began to show, far to the west. Immediately, we started towing down toward the takeoff site. No other sailplane had moved toward the line; any sophisticate would have known it was too early to stay up. Phil Easley taxied over in Dave Johnson's Super Cub for the tow. "Let us know if there's anything up there," he said. The request was fair. I had not yet seen a dust devil, but west-southwest along the road to Monahans the smoke at the carbon plant began to stir. It was moving up into the air—an unfailing sign of thermal activity, because every evening, through the night and until instability begins next day, the plant makes a silent black ribbon of carbon smoke which moves close over the ground.

I was fairly relaxed. Beebo was not in a hurry; Phil Easley was ready, but thought there was plenty of time. Only Ruth was in a desperate hurry to get the flight started. She pushed and pushed. Earlier she had put on the yarn yaw indicator, and for a lark had written YAW INDI-CATOR on the piece of masking tape which held it to the canopy. Now, under her pressure, I got into the cockpit, fixed the shoulder harness and seat belt, put on the knee-board, and took in the water and other luxuries. Controls were tested a final time; the canopy was pulled overhead, fastened and sealed; the towrope was connected, release checked, and fastened again. "Raise the tip," I shouted to John who was running my wingtip for me. Ahead, the Super Cub moved and slack worked out of the rope. Phil wagged the Cub's tail, and I answered by wagging the tail of *Cirro-Q*. The flight was ready.

There was an intermittent scraping of the steel shoe against concrete on the runway, then it became steady; then the sound of an accelerating wheel as we began to roll and the keel leaving the runway as full back-stick was pulled. A moment later we were airborne. It was 11:50. Three hundred feet off the ground, I remembered I had not turned on the barograph. Damn!! In a rage I threw myself forward, compressed my left arm into half its usual dimensions, managed to get it to slide back into the rear compartment and groped for the brass wire which controlled the starting lever. I found it and pulled back. Was it on? There was too much air noise to hear any ticking. At four hundred feet, I got back my arm.

"Eight Nine Nine Ground, this is Eight Nine Nine Air. Do you read? Over."

"Eight Nine Nine Air, this is Eight Nine Nine Ground. I read you loud and clear, over." The calm steady voice of Ruth Petry.

"Eight Nine Nine Ground, this is Air. I forgot to turn the barograph on. Will you see Licher right away and see if this trace will be all right. I got it on about 350 feet in the air. If it isn't O. K., I'll land right away."

"Eight Nine Nine Air, Roger. I'll call you back in a few minutes."

The tow went on, and we gained altitude slowly, flying around the field in a big circle. At 1800 feet, I released in what seemed to be a 500 foot-a-minute thermal because we were now going up at over 700 fpm. A dive was made to 1500 feet to make a good notch, then I tried to find the lift. The best available was 100 feet which was used as we drifted out on course. For some time the radio was silent. Ten minutes later we were up at 2500 feet about three miles downwind of the field. Not good enough. I headed home, losing altitude quite rapidly. On the way back Ruth Petry's voice came in again.

"Eight Nine Nine Air, this is Eight Nine Nine Ground, do you read? Over."

"Roger. I read you loud and clear. Over."

"Eight Nine Nine Air, I saw Lloyd Licher*, and he said the trace would be all right as long as you have a good notch on it showing release altitude."

"Roger. Thanks a lot. If you see him again, tell him I towed to 1800 feet and made a dive to 1500 for the notch. He has this year's calibration paper for my barograph. I gained a thousand feet, but it wasn't good enough to leave in. Now I'm back down below two thousand, getting close to the field. I haven't hit a bump. There's a good chance I'll be down again in a few minutes."

We covered the rest of the distance back to the field and got over the southwest corner at 1400 feet when I hit a strong bump; thirty seconds later we had a thermal centered. It showed steady 500 foot lift. I made a radio call to the car asking them to stand by; things were looking up. The lift carried to 7500 feet, 4500 above terrain.

"Eight Nine Nine Ground, this is Eight Nine Nine Air. I'm at 7500. Heading out on course. I'd suggest you leave as soon as possible. That thermal was a good steady 500. With the tail wind, I should be moving right along."

"Roger Eight Nine Nine Air. I'll move out as soon as I get some sandwiches for the boys."

Five hundred feet per minute; cruise 80 miles per hour indicated, about 85 actual. Plus the tail wind; ten knots—about 95. Divide by two for circling time: 47½. Call it 45. Let's see; that should put us a little beyond Monahans at the hour. No, that doesn't account for the tow and the time lost in going back to the field once. O. K. Close to Monahans. The clouds over there look very good now. Nothing between here and there though, except some weak,

---

* Executive Secretary of The Soaring Society of America who processes all barograph traces for C Legs and Records.

watery cumulus. Only three of them in all. We can try
one. What are you worrying about? You climbed out at
500 feet a minute. You released in the bottom of a thermal
good for 500. There will be plenty between here and Monahans. Hell yes. Altitude to burn. Why didn't any of the
experts decide to go west today? Shut up you idiot. Fly
the sailplane.

The ground below slipped past quickly as I steered
a little south of southwest to get over the road, Highway
80, going to Monahans, Pecos, Toyah, Kent, Van Horn,
Sierra Blanca, and the Goal. In just a few minutes I got
over the road and changed course to west-southwest. One
of the three watery clouds had already been tried and was
completely dead. We were getting uncomfortably low,
almost down to 2000, and worked some 150 foot lift. After
five minutes of this, I headed out again—this time at low
speed to get the maximum glide angle—and passed over
the smoke from the carbon plant. The black smoke en-
couraged things a little. From 1800 feet we encountered
a slow but steady lift. We got back up to 3000 feet above
terrain, then hit a sinker. For some time there was no
chance to cruise. We circled and circled; out of any immediate danger of a landing, but too low to proceed. One
hour after takeoff, I was only six miles beyond Penwell, a
miserable twenty-two miles out, and this with a good tail
wind. At this rate, it would take almost ten hours.

A couple of miles farther on, we passed over a road
leading off into endless distance to the south. Ahead, lay
our own road with its railroad paralleling. Behind lay the
short distance I had come, under thin cirrus overcast.
Ahead, getting closer now, were the glorious cumuli that
looked like Texas at its best. Spread out below was the
mighty Permian Basin, one of the richest oil fields in Texas,
with its derricks, lengths of steel well-casing, corrugated
iron shacks, and the low scrub growth stretching to the

horizon. Each plant had a wind-drifted hummock of sand
at its base. No inviting place to land a sailplane. Just past
the road we hit an unexpected thermal, the second good
one of the day, and went up to 8000 feet. This altitude was
used up getting past the thirty-mile mark after which we
came over much better terrain. There were large open
areas which appeared to be dry lakes. Then I got low again
and saw they were sand dunes, with waves too steep and
close together for safe landing. An area of gentle sink
followed the dunes and presently we were in range of the
airport at Monahans. But no thought was given to the airport because just half a mile farther was the first great
cumulus of the day. Ahead lay fast lift, fast cruising speeds,
and soaring from cloudbase to cloudbase far above the
earth.

The town of Monahans was passed with about 5000
feet in hand, 2400 above the ground; then the airport, 38
miles out, still with 2250 feet. I pressed on. Then, almost
under the cloud came 600 foot a minute sink; it went to
800 fpm down. I looked frantically from the cloud to the
airport and back. The altimeter gave us 1600 feet above
ground; I tapped it and read only 1400. The airport was
close, but against the wind and beyond violent sink. I
remembered the time at Bishop when the glide angle to
landing was 7 to 1, all the way down from 15,000 feet. The
cloud *had* to have good lift, but I was in what should have
been the column of rising air. The airport; the cloud; and
nothing to land on directly below. Fifteen seconds more
passed—then at 1200 feet sudden zero sink, and immediately afterward strong lift. We flew well into it before starting
the turn. It was an extremely rough thermal which threw
Cirro-Q about like a cork, but we started climbing at 600
feet a minute. Soon it was a solid 1000 feet and carried right
up to cloudbase at 9700, by far the greatest altitude of the
day. We were 40 miles out and set course for Pyote Air

Force Base indicating over 80 miles per hour. I called Ruth Petry and reported the new state of affairs. Ahead there was almost fifty percent sky cover of live towering cumuli, and we were heading into the area almost seven thousand feet above ground. We had bridged the long, difficult area without cloud. The first part of the flight was over.

Ruth and the trailer fell behind now as the cruising speed was high and steady. No lift was worked which did not approximate 1000 feet a minute. I climbed up to base and headed on course. At Pyote we crossed back to the north side of the road to fly under a short cloudstreet. Two hours out, I had come sixty-four miles. Pecos was only ten miles ahead and the speed average had gone up from 22 to 32 miles an hour. Only a little over half an hour in this lift and look what has happened, I thought. With another hour the average should be up over 40. That would bring us to Kent where the road turns straight west and runs 40 miles in that direction to Van Horn, 160 miles out. Even being conservative, we should make Van Horn in two hours and another hour to put the Goal in sight. Three hours to final glide.

Pecos went by and fell quickly behind. I called on the radio and noticed their signal was getting weak; they were far back. Toyah was the next village, fifteen miles ahead. Can we do it in fifteen minutes? Far ahead I could see mountains on the horizon for the first time, the Apache Mountains north of course and the Davis Mountains a little south. Off to the southwest of Kent was a butte called Boracho Peak. Also ahead there was an ominous lessening of cloud. In the district of Toyah there was only 35 percent cover; at Kent less than 10 percent and the cumuli there had weak bases and very little development. The weatherman had called for widely scattered thunderstorms out here this afternoon. It looks like a hell of a poor start for thunderstorm weather, I thought. We did not make

Toyah in fifteen minutes, or even twenty. Lift went down to 500 feet a minute under exceptionally good clouds; a few gave less than 200 fpm, and sometimes it was hard to reach cloudbase. After passing the town, we made a first detour around a dry hole in the clouds. The throttle was pulled in; I began cruising at 60.

"Eight Nine Nine Ground, this is Eight Nine Nine Air, do you read? Over."

"Eight Nine Nine Air, this is Eight Nine Nine Ground. Reading you loud and clear. Over." Her voice was strong again. She had almost caught up with me.

"Eight Nine Nine Ground, I'm ten miles beyond Toyah, about 105 miles out. I've had to detour around a hole in cloud over the road. Now I'm coming back in, but lift is decreasing steadily. Ahead it doesn't look too good. What is your position? Over."

"Roger Eight Nine Nine Air. We're just coming out of Toyah. We have been travelling fast, but could not keep up with you for a while, over."

"I'll call again in a few minutes if things change. Present altitude is only sixty-five hundred. Air out."

"Ground out."

Things changed, but not for the better. I tried two clouds which must have been dying; they had no lift. There was moderate sink on the way to others. I left the road in search of something better. It was not to be found, so we flew back. Three hours after takeoff, we were 108 miles out where the railroad separates briefly from the highway before they come together again at Kent. Ruth had caught up in the Ranch Wagon and trailer; they were on my left, not two thousand feet below. A little over half the distance to the Goal had been covered. Now, just before 3:00 P. M., it should have been the height of the day and prospects of success were fading.

"Eight Nine Nine Ground, this is Eight Nine Nine Air. I'm right beside you at less than two thousand feet. Stand by. If the flight goes on, I will have to get some new lift pretty soon. Air out."

"Roger. Eight Nine Nine Ground."

New lift came, fairly steady at 200 to 300 feet a minute. The railroad was almost four miles away, but converging again when I passed over the junction of Highways 80 and 290 where we had turned off last year on our way to the Meet at Georgetown. I saw a pretty lake, north of the railroad, just before it rejoined our road. Then they both passed over culverts, bent to the right, and went straight west into Kent where Harland Ross had started his big flight just four days ago. For a surprising amount of time things held up quite well. We passed Kent and the next little step was Baracho Station, on a line between Boracho Peak and the Apache Mountains. The little cruising we did was now all at maximum glide. Each new thermal did not go quite as high as the last one. It seemed hours since we had been at cloudbase. The road below was now passing over high ground, all above 4000 feet. I made Baracho Station and turned left one hundred and thirty-five miles out. Two miles south of the road I saw a building cloud. We came under it only 1100 feet above the ground and got nothing better than zero sink. Two and a half miles north was a marginal landing place in the grassy bottom of a creek bed. The problem would be to thread our way between horses and cows grazing there. Half a mile west there was a low ridge. I made a call to Ruth, and she stopped the car and trailer. There was nothing much to do but watch the dying struggle.

Zero sink! Eleven hundred feet heading for the ridge. 200 fpm down on the Memphis. Easy right turn. Keep the yarn centered, and 45 mph. North heading now with the road in the near distance, just a little way below. They're

parked beside the road. I can see the two boys. Memphis
at zero. Tap the altimeter; 1025 feet above the deck. Can't
make it like this. A sudden burst of lift: 600 fpm, and the
airspeed is up to 65. Quick back pressure on the stick; a
zoom, then forward again to keep speed at 45. Tap altimeter: 1100 again! Stay with it. You aren't dead yet. East
in the turn shows Kent in the distance, fifteen miles back.
Then south, looking at the Davis Mountains. Thirty miles
away over Mt. Livermore is the beginning of a line of
superb cumulus cloud. It runs west-northwest to the horizon. If you could gain seven thousand feet you might make
it. Quit dreaming. From here you could only do a fifth of
the distance even if there were no sink on the way. We're
lower than Boracho Peak, and it's only 1400 feet above
the road. Keep that yarn centered. The green pellet is a
little off, but the Memphis is on zero again. West, looking
at the ridge. No closer. The wind must have died. Altitude?
1125. Not bad, not bad. If there were only some place to
land when this quits. Below is a shaggy desert like Tombstone. Quit thinking of that crackup. You can make it to
the creek bed. The worst that can happen is busting up
the ship a little. Then no Diamond this year. 300 fpm sink.
500 fpm sink. Tap altimeter: 980 feet. Boom! 1000 fpm
climb. Is this a thermal? Pull up quick. Get back the altitude you lost. Three seconds and the climb is gone. Altimeter? 1075. Now a steady 50 fpm climb . . .

The road and trailer in view; the creekbed over the
fence. Now east toward Kent; south looking at the magnificent and unreachable cumuli; west again. Altimeter? 1025.
No good. You lost fifty feet in that circle. North: 700 fpm
climb. Straighten out a minute. Maybe there is something
over this way. 400 fpm climb. Better. Way better. Now
turn sharp. Altimeter: 1150. Good. East: zero sink. Now 300
fpm down. Steady all over at 300 fpm down. South. The
row of cumulus clouds again. What was the torture of

155

Tantalus? Having a bunch of grapes held just out of reach? Whoever wrote that never flew a sailplane and looked at cumuli he would never reach. West again. The ridge no closer. Still half a mile away, so there's no wind at all down here. No ridge soaring either. The clouds? Very widely scattered, tiny, so thin there is no darkness at the bottom, you can almost see through them. The bottoms are not flat; the tops are not hard; no vertical development. Great day for a picnic. Oh *God,* for one of those Texas thermals you hear so much about. A while ago you were nervous when you got down as low as two thousand feet; now wondering if you'll ever get up that high again. You forgot to tap the altimeter heading west that time. Did you gain or lose? Zero now heading north; 50 fpm up heading east; 150 fpm down going south; west toward the ridge now. Altimeter: 1040. Where did I lose all that? The steady sink after the last burst of lift. That's it. Another circle. All 40 fpm down. 1020 heading toward the ridge . . . Another one . . . The same . . . 1000 feet high pointing at the ridge. Then another tremendous momentary burst of lift; stick back, zoom, forward now. 45 mph again. Altimeter: 1160. That was a big one. Let's get the earphones on again. Hey, watch what you're doing. Center that yarn. Airspeed up to 45. You can't afford to lose fifty feet in a stall. Where's a dust devil? God, *God,* let's have a dust devil.

My shirt and forehead were soaked in sweat; the tension was becoming unbearable as it is just before violence; in the back of the mind were shadowy pictures of a broken sailplane and being pinned under wreckage—in agony from the dreaded spinal compression fracture.

"Eight Nine Nine Ground, this is Eight Nine Nine Air, do you read? Over."

"EIGHT NINE NINE AIR, THIS IS EIGHT NINE NINE . . ." They were less than two miles away, and I had not turned the volume down. It almost blew me out of the cockpit.

"Eight Nine Nine Ground, this is Air. I've been working this stuff at zero for several minutes without gaining or losing anything. How is the road or that creek bed for a landing?"

"Eight Nine Nine Air, the road is wide enough, but you will have to miss a few of these posts marking culverts. You can roll off to the side without any trouble because the north shoulder is very wide."

"Roger. Stand by. Have you seen any dust devils?" I asked.

"No. There haven't been any around here since we stopped."

"Roger. I'll stand by the radio. If you see anything in range, holler. I've only got a thousand feet."

Five minutes went by. Then ten and fifteen. All the while, altitude varied from 950 to 1200 feet above ground. It was necessary to get the most out of each gust in order to maintain altitude because the greater part of every circle was in sink. After each promising burst of lift an adjustment was made in the circle and the center of the turn wandered about like a sleepwalker. From the ground, soaring appears effortless and graceful, I remembered crazily. After nineteen minutes the variometer began to show steady lift; the needle was above zero all the way around. Very slowly the ground began to get farther away. Fifteen miles off to west-northwest a fairly good cumulus cloud was building, the first encouraging sign in almost an hour . . .

"Eight Nine Nine Ground, I now have almost three thousand feet. I'm heading on course again. This thermal doesn't have any more lift. Keep me in sight if you can. I'll be flying at max. glide."

"Roger, Eight Nine Nine Air."

We passed over the ridge I had spent so much time looking at, then over a side road and a dry creek. Five miles past the ridge we were 143 miles out. We had been in reduced sink and had lost only a few hundred feet after leaving the top of our saving thermal. As I came back north toward the road, we flew by Plateau Station on the right. Eight miles ahead lay Wild Horse Station. Then came the sickening disappointment of a wide area of heavy sink. It did not feel like the momentary sink which is on the outside of a strong thermal; it was more as if the air had suddenly vanished and we were falling unsupported through space, like an automobile driven at high speed over a cliff. 500 fpm down, a steady 500 fpm down. With sink of this kind, there *must* be lift somewhere, I thought, but after going through it for two minutes, we were down below 1500 feet, and another minute brought us under 1000. A few miles ahead lay Wild Horse Station. I made a 180 degree right turn and was over the road at 800 feet, still coming down 500 feet a minute.

"Eight Nine Nine Ground, this is Air. I'm coming in. Don't see any place to land except the road. How is it there? Over." Desperately.

"Eight Nine Nine Air, this is Ground. It's good right here, but watch out for the wires passing over the road. I'll stop the car by them to mark it. Also watch out for . . ."

I turned the radio off because there was no time for any more warnings. The problem was to land on the road in an easterly direction, missing the overhead wires Ruth had spoken about; missing any culvert marker posts that might be there to rip off a wing, landing between cars which were going east and touching down just after a car going west had passed by—then rolling off before the next car could get to the landing spot. At the present rate of descent, there were ninety seconds to go from 750 feet, a little more, because descent rate lessens close to the ground but then I would probably use the spoilers. Nerves were like a fishline stretched taut and shaking, just a hair below the point where it breaks.

All that work for this, not even a hundred and fifty miles, I thought bitterly. Forty miles of tiptoe flying, then the good stuff, then weakening again and that hole back there I barely crawled out of. Then you sink right into the ground. Another failure. Have you heard the latest, they will say. He couldn't hit a goal in Arizona so he came all the way to Texas. *Odessa,* Texas, mind you. God knows how many times he tried it, and he never came really close. *No,* you aren't serious are you? Couldn't hit a goal even at *Odessa?* Amazing. He should have kept the Baby Bowlus.

At 700 feet came an unexpected bump, then another one strong enough to make zero sink. I banked steeply to the right. After one circle we were still at 700. Another circle brought us out with 720; a third circle found us at 760. I turned on the radio again.

"Eight Nine Nine Ground, this is Air. I have some weak lift which started at seven hundred feet. If my nerves hold out I'll try to work it up."

"Roger Eight Nine Nine Air. We'll stand by."

A few more circles got us back to a thousand feet after which the thermal strengthened, and we climbed steadily at 200 feet a minute. It lasted more than ten minutes, and we climbed well over three thousand feet above terrain. When the lift stopped, instead of going straight west on course, I headed a little northward toward a cloud which appeared strong enough to have lift. The first minutes of the cruise were timid and full of fear—expecting any second to hit violent sink which presently would end the flight. But this time, there was a difference. We had come within gliding range of Culberson County Airport, just east of Van Horn, no matter how bad the sink. I flew by Wild

159

Horse Station and went on; the sink never came. When we got under the cloud, we were still almost three thousand feet high and the cloud added another five hundred. Heading toward the airport, for the first time in over an hour there was a chance to relax.

In a very short time, the airport went by, three thousand feet below, and I had to fight off a strong temptation to land there—the first time in my life I had been tempted to land purposely, far short of a Goal. What a beautiful airport it was! Those wide, wide asphalt strips, one of them six thousand feet long, with no marker posts, no wires, no fences, no hummocks, no cattle, no rocks, no cars.

Over Van Horn were weak clouds, and at the immediate edge of town, a dirt landing strip. Off to the north stretched the long Sierra Diablo, Spanish for Devil Range, with Victoria Peak jutting a point into the sky twenty miles away. Four miles west of Van Horn the road turned half right and the course changed from west by south to west-northwest, and thirty miles along the road nestled the town of Sierra Blanca, just twenty-one miles from the Goal. Southward lay the long, slender Quitman Mountains, with their southern tail almost in the Rio Grande River. Much closer, just seventeen miles southwest of Van Horn, was Eagle Peak, the summit of which was 7500 feet above sea level, the same as my present altitude, 3500 feet above Van Horn, and over Eagle Peak were small but strong cumuli. South of Eagle Peak and not very far beyond, was the row of mighty cumulonimbus clouds, now only a little over half as far away as it had been when we were almost down, just north of Boracho Peak. They were over the southern extremity of the Van Horn Mountains, less than twenty miles away, straight south. Reaching Van Horn I began to work for altitude and called Ruth. She had beaten me into the town and had been waiting for a call. The boys needed food; the car needed gasoline and time to cool off, having overheated during the two periods when it was parked by the road and left running to keep the radio going. I said I would call again in fifteen minutes, then signed off.

The altitude did not come. We got back up to 3500 feet above the town and stopped. For twenty minutes I worked in a number of places and stayed within three hundred feet of this level, during which time I muttered a good many unprintable comments about Texas thermals. Westward on course, the sky had very widely scattered and almost transparent cumuli, just like the ones from Baracho Station to Wild Horse Station. South, within possible reach in dead air, but far beyond range in sink, lay small and solid cumuli before the area of giant cumulonimbus. The great row of cloud seemed to generate without pause, because it looked exactly as it had an hour before. There was no rain, no cirrus anvil-tops blowing off, no weakening of any kind. Flying toward the Goal in dead air, I could perhaps make another twenty miles from this altitude, maybe a little more, and hope for very improbable thermals. It was getting too late for more last minute saves. Flying west would bring me within Silver C distance of the Goal. But the closer you get and fail, the more agonizing it is. Going south and heading for the big clouds, I would stay over fifty miles from the Goal, at least for the first sixteen miles, and might very well go down in sink before getting to them. It would be like making an end run in football when you fear being outrun by the opposing backs. Going straight ahead seemed like a center plunge from the thirty-five yard line, on last down, with eight yards to go. To the south, cloudbase was very high and dark, indicating strong lift. Westward, toward my Goal, the sky looked like defeat. A straight line is the shortest distance between two points? This is *soaring*, not geometry. If you fight it out all the way you can always face yourself, but

161

Soaring

let's fight it out with a little intelligence, not just guts.

Thus came the decision to head south. I called Ruth and did not raise her. Five minutes later I called again and she still did not answer. We headed out, still 3500 feet above terrain. There are two roads leading south from Van Horn, one going a little east of south, the other west of straight south—like the supports of a teeter-totter, which was Highway 80 and the parallel railroad we had come in over. I took the one heading west of south which angled ever so slightly toward the Goal. Ahead on my left were the Van Horn Mountains; on the right was Eagle Peak. Ahead below were two ranches with wide green fields which would be suitable for landing. I called Ruth a third time, got her, and told her of my decision and where to look if she lost contact. As soon as I left Van Horn, we began sinking 125 feet a minute, *Cirro-Q's* minimum rate of sink in dead air. The ground approached; the cumuli got closer. With so many variables in the formula, I could not tell early in the glide if we had enough altitude to stay aloft until we got to the first lift. The second part of the flight had been flown.

Ten minutes can seem like a long time when it is in a glide without any trace of lift and the glide is started a little too low. We flew over the road, losing 125 feet a minute. Eight miles from Van Horn the road lost its arrow-like straightness and made a tiny jog to the right, then left, ran across a stream, crossed the Southern Pacific Railroad and a parallel highway, then bent left in a slow curve and ran south alongside an intermittently used spur which ran to Micolithic, a mining camp on the western slope of the Van Horn Mountains. The road south of the railway paralleled it for eight miles northwest to the village of Hot Wells. From there the railroad went straight toward Sierra Blanca where it joined the road and rail line from Van Horn. At my left there was a settlement named Collado

162

on the railway. Beside it were good fields, but now I was very close to the first cumulus and still 2200 feet above the ground. On the other side, a third of the way from my position to Hot Wells, lay a ranch with more good landing fields. Ten miles straight West jutted the summit of Eagle Peak. I left the intersection, headed southwest for the cumuli and hoped. We were more than 1400 feet below the summit of Eagle Peak. There was no tenseness as there had been the other times because landing areas were plentiful, but the variometer was as dead as if *Cirro-Q* were on the ground in a windless night. We had come all this way at maximum glide; the red pellet in the Cosim looked as if it were struck—two feet per second down; even the Memphis variometer needle scarcely moved. We flew under the first little cloud and nothing happened, even though it looked strong. Still 2000 feet over the ground, but now there was an air of peace and finality in the glide. Ship and pilot had both done their best. It was not enough. The small cumuli outside the edges of the cumulonimbus mass had enticed us into making a decision and an experiment. It failed. There was no lift under them. Chalk up one more.

Then everything changed. The air came to life with unbelievable suddenness. A heavy sink was followed almost at once by a wide area of lift, and we began to climb 200 feet a minute. After circling eight minutes we had regained the lost altitude and were back up level with the top of Eagle Peak, as high as we had been since before getting to Kent, so long ago. This time the lift went on, and we climbed to 9000 feet, almost a mile above ground. From here I set a course west-northwest over the mountain, and even the gigantic boulders at the summit looked harmless from the new altitude. I looked ahead wistfully and wondered if we could get back on the course at Sierra Blanca. The clouds there were lifeless little shreds, without form or power. We were now almost 180 miles out, but

Soaring

I was not thinking of glide angles. I thought about getting back on course. As it happened, there were two folds in the chart in this area, and it was very difficult to look ahead and get an accurate picture of the overall terrain because you cannot open a chart up in the narrow cockpit of *Cirro-Q*, and we were too far off course for the mileage markers to give an accurate estimate of the distance remaining to the Goal.

Ninety degrees to my left are the great cumulonimbus, I thought. From here they look like they're in easy range, no matter what kind of sink there is in between. Or shall I go straight toward the Goal from here? Or get back on the road? No. There will probably be sink, and we still have to cross the Quitman Mountains. We have come ten miles south-southwest from Van Horn, then fourteen miles west-northwest. Now, to get under the cumulonimbus clouds, we will have to go south and gain nothing toward the Goal. This is like tacking in a sailboat. Where do we come out? Looks like the best cloud is over the south end of Quitman Mountain, only three or four miles from the Rio Grande River. I think that's it. O. K. Holler at Ruth and let's go.

"Eight Nine Nine Ground, this is Eight Nine Nine Air. I'm over the northwest end of Eagle Peak a little above eight thousand feet. Now I'm heading south toward the river. The lift looks very good there, and I think I can make it. If we lose contact, look for me around Indian Hot Springs. That's a town on the Rio Grande a few miles south of the end of the Quitman Mountains. There's a road that goes in there from Sierra Blanca. Do you have all that? Over."

After we talked back and forth a minute, Ruth understood everything and told me she was halfway between Van Horn and Sierra Blanca, the last town she would go through before reaching the Goal. I headed south, a little

164

The Author and Cirro-Q.

From the Cockpit of Cirro-Q.

under 50 miles an hour for best glide. There were about twelve miles to go before reaching the lower end of the Quitman Mountains, under the great cloud, near the river. We had four thousand feet to use. On the new course the air died once again, and we sank 120 to 130 feet a minute. Then, after crossing a road halfway to the point of expected lift, the sink increased. After flying through most of the open area between the small cumuli that got us over Eagle Peak and the great clouds ahead, we still had 2000 feet, half the original altitude, but very little to spare in a pinch. Then came heavy sink again. We lost 300 feet in less than a minute, but this time I did not worry too much. I thought we were getting close. The southern end of the low Quitman Ridge was just ahead when, after a minute of violent sink, the needle of the Memphis variometer moved upward in a majestic arc. From 600 fpm down, it climbed toward zero, then beyond—to 300, 500, 800, then a solid 1000 fpm climb while I could feel the strong power under wings. When we began to circle, the variometer indicated almost a thousand foot a minute climb all the way around. The circling was continued and every minute put another thousand feet of air below *Cirro-Q* and me. There was a feeling of triumph which can only be experienced by a sailpilot who has found strong lift after a long, desperate struggle close to the ground. I circled up as the Quitman Range fell away below, and I could now view the Sierra Diablo and Mount Livermore, far to the east under shadow from the beginning of this row of great cumuli; then the Sierra Vieja and the long, long slender thread of the Rio Grande River, shining under the late afternoon sun and coming from the far northwest where it flowed through El Paso. And the rapid climb went on as we got above 10,000 feet, the highest point of the day so far. Then eleven thousand and twelve, until we touched the mist at cloudbase, 12,400 feet high, almost 9000 above Esperanza

—and though I did not know it at the time because of the folds in the chart, McCoy Field was now only thirty-three miles away.

The line of cloud pointed almost straight at my Goal and for the first distance, it was a nearly solid cloudstreet. I headed on course, a course which gradually took us away from the Quitman Ridge and toward the river. In a few minutes, I flew beyond a fold in the chart and came over the tiny corner of a last panel before being on the fold which marked the Goal. We had flown west of Sierra Blanca and were half way between the upper length of the Quitman Ridge and the Rio Grande.

"Eight Nine Nine Ground, this is Eight Nine Nine Air, Do you read? Over."

"Eight Nine Nine Air, this is Ground. Reading you loud and clear. Over."

"Eight Nine Nine Ground, I'm south by west from Sierra Blanca between the mountain and the river. I'm at twelve thousand three hundred feet and cruising toward the Goal under a cloudstreet. This time I'll permit myself a little optimism. What is your position? Over."

"Eight Nine Nine Air, we are just beyond the town of Sierra Blanca. I'll go right on to the Goal as fast as I can. Over."

"Roger. I'll give you a call in fifteen minutes. Air out."

"Ground out."

I passed over the last fold in the chart as we came to the end of the cloudstreet. I had been miserly in the extreme with my altitude, and had never put the speed up over 60. Once I had even stopped to circle when we got below twelve thousand feet. We still had 12,000 and now the Goal was only nineteen miles away. Half way along the final run there was now a single towering cumulus cloud. Ahead, on the Mexican side of the Rio Grande was the town of Banderas, then on the American side, Fort Quit-

man, then Providencia on the Mexican side, and McCoy
Field on our side, between the river and Highway 80,
where the road turns northwest to parallel the river all
the way into El Paso. On the chart there was no mention
of Esperanza, only the legend:

(McCoy, 3500--19) and the purple O indicating a
small field. 3500 feet? We have 12,000, that leaves 8500 to
work with. Out away from cloud and with no big mountains around, there isn't very likely to be heavy sink. 8500
feet? Yes, 8500! Call it 7500. In dead air that should take
you forty-five miles. How far do we have to go now?

At ten mile intervals all along the original course I
had marked the chart with red ink numbers indicating the
distance from Odessa. The first mileage number on this
last fold of the chart was 200. By road it was 213 miles
from Odessa to the Goal. Even approaching the Goal as
we were from miles south of the course, I estimated our
distance away could not be over 17 miles. And altitude
enough to go 45! As I was hunting for the town of Fort
Quitman on the river, we flew under the last cloud which
had moderate lift, and we circled briefly. I could not see
Fort Quitman, but Providencia was in the right place, just
south of a left jog in the river. Ten miles upstream, there
was another left jog. I found it. McCoy is on the right side,
two thirds of the way up between the jogs, closer to the
road than the river . . .

It was not there!

We flew closer to the Goal at a mile a minute and the
whole position was rechecked—the two jogs in the river,
ten miles apart; the road from Sierra Blanca, first approaching the river at a 45 degree angle, then curving right and
passing over a concrete bridge, and the continued approach
to the river at an angle of 25 degrees; then a second bridge
and the road turning northwest, parallel with the river as
they both vanished in the distance toward El Paso. It was

all there. Everything checked out, but McCoy Field which was missing. This is great, I thought. You are always hearing about discontinued fields. Quickly I turned over the chart to find out the date of publication even though I knew I had bought it just for this trip. March 12, 1959. Only five months old. That's no help. We flew over Providencia and the first jog in the river, only five miles from the Goal. Five happy minutes later, I made a long turn over McCoy Field, or where it should be, and we were still more than a mile above ground.

Now that we were straight over the place, I studied the area again. Close to the river, there were many good fields and finding a safe place to land was no problem, but would this count as a successful goal flight when I had specified McCoy Field? Very close to the spot where the field was supposed to be, there was an area stripped of vegetation. Earlier I had dismissed it as a wide gravel creek bottom. Now, I observed from the drainage pattern that there was no creek going that way. It did not look like a strip, being in the shape of a slender wedge rather than the usual rectangle, but I knew it was not an arroyo. A dirt road came off the highway, forked, and one of the branches ran through the open area, then twisted down what appeared to be a hill, ran between buildings and joined another small road close to the river. After looking at the wedge for some time, I decided it must be the strip. Its narrow end looked all right for most aircraft, but not wide enough for the fifty foot span of *Cirro-Q*.

"Eight Nine Nine Ground, this is Eight Nine Nine Air. Do you read? Over."

"Roger, Eight Nine Nine Air. Reading loud and clear. Over."

"Eight Nine Nine Ground, I'm over the Goal and have several thousand feet of altitude left. What is your position? Over."

169

"Roger. Let's see. We're about fifteen miles beyond Sierra Blanca."

I hunted for the car and trailer, then spotted them less than two miles from the first bridge where the road curved.

"Do you see a right turn in the road coming up, about a mile and a half ahead, then a bridge?"

"Roger. I do," she answered.

"The turnoff to the field is about two miles past that bridge. I'll guide you in."

The next ten minutes were very improbable as the sailplane gave directions to the crew. I told Ruth where to turn, which fork in the road to take, then asked how the field looked after she had driven over it. She described the deep gully at the upper end, how wide the strip was at the narrow end, the amount of incline and the height of the strip above the green fields on the valley floor. Then came the matter of witneses to the landing. There should be two adults.

"Can you stay up there a while?" she asked.

"Yes. I have plenty of altitude. Just in case it takes you all day, I'll go hunt for a thermal."

Two minutes later came the report that she had found someone, but he could not speak English. He sent her to "La Tienda." She went farther down the hill and found a general store and post office combination run by Mrs. Ray McCoy, who was kind enough to close up so she could witness the landing. Then back up the hill in triumph came Ruth with the car and trailer, John, Gregory, Beebo, and Mrs. McCoy. I had been aloft over six hours.

After several minutes of acrobatic stunting to lose altitude and celebrate the end of the day, I made a pass three hundred feet above and to one side of the field to get a close look, then pulled up and went out over the wide valley at a hundred miles an hour while *Cirro-Q's* wings gayly cut the air. The valley looked like an undiscovered spot in Paradise: green, full of timeless peace; the row of cumulonimbus, with some of the tops now blowing off in anvils, had begun to drift southward into Mexico. I turned on base leg close to the river as my speed wore off and made a last turn into final approach. I held off until we got over the wide part of the strip. Then touchdown and landing roll with the keel soon digging granite and dust. When we stopped, there was only the ticking of the barograph with a snap every six seconds as the stylus punched paper, strangely quiet after six hours and ten minutes of air noise.

I sat for a long moment, very quiet and happy, and touched the sides of my lovely three Diamond sailplane. Then I opened the canopy, unfastened the shoulder harness and seat belt, pulled up my stiff legs, and climbed out of the cockpit—a Diamond C pilot: Arizona's first, number fifteen in the United States, the one hundred and seventeenth in the world. Ruth Petry drove up to shake my hand. She had a grin that went from Esperanza to Odessa, and the two boys and Beebo jumped out of the Ranch Wagon. It was a time of great emotion.

There was a feeling of ceremony in everything I did, because each thing was now done for the first time as a Diamond Pilot. The unstiffening of legs, the first can of beer which Ruth had thoughtfully provided, and eating the ice cold watermelon which Mrs. McCoy had brought up the hill.

Evening was coming on by the time *Cirro-Q* was back on the trailer. The clouds which had brought us to the Goal had drifted twenty or thirty miles down into Mexico. One of them showed an occasional flash of lightning. Inside my chest was the warmth and glow of victory, the strongest it had been since that day three years before when I landed the Baby Albatross in another Texas field and listened

171

to the ticking of the same barograph, the Peravia I had bought from E. J. Reeves, on the day I won my Silver C.

Across the road from the McCoy store at Esperanza, there is a wooden bridge which goes over an inactive channel of the Rio Grande. I walked across it alone and bent down to pick up a handful of the dust of Texas, then watched it slowly run between my fingers; part of the warm earth where I had met June and Wally Wiberg, Oats Schwartzenburger, Al Backstrom, Jon Carsey, and Dick Johnson, and E. J. Reeves. To the east lay the range of low mountains that *Cirro-Q* and I had flown over on the last part of our trip to the Goal, silently disappearing now in the dusk. I turned west and the sun was down below the horizon.

Then I raised my eyes and looked once again at the sky.

DIAMOND C PLAQUE,
SMITHSONIAN INSTITUTION
International Numbers in Parentheses

1. (1) John Robinson
2. (4) J. Shelly Charles*
3. (7) Paul F. Bikle
4. (8) Raymon H. Parker
5. (9) William S. Ivans, Jr.
6. (10) Paul R. Opitz
7. (81) Graham S. Thomson
8. (82) Robert E. Brown
9. (83) Lyle A. Maxey
10. (84) Dewey J. Mancuso
11. (85) Sterling V. Starr
12. (97) Robert F. Symons*
13. (113) Robert Lee Moore
14. (116) Harland C. Ross
15. (117) Joseph C. Lincoln
16. (140) John D. Ryan
17. (184) Robert F. Litle, Jr.
18. (238) Marcel Godinat
19. (239) Rudolph T. Allemann
20. (256) Jack H. Lambie
21. (253) Edwin D. McClanahan, Jr.
22. (255) Richard E. Schreder
23. (320) Jack J. Arkovich
24. (318) Carlin W. Brinkmann, Sr.
25. (323) Kai Gertsen
26. (324) Benjamin W. Greene
27. (332) George Arents, Jr.
28. (333) Wylie H. Mullen, Jr.
29. (335) Jerry D. Robertson
30. (359) Dale S. May
31. (366) John W. Williams
32. (367) Leslie J. Benis
33. (370) Richard H. Johnson
34. (372) Dr. Hartmut Schmidt
35. (373) Neal H. Ridenour
36. (376) James W. Leland
37. (377) Philip R. Miller
38. (378) Bruce Beebe
39. (391) David C. Johnson
40. (399) Carl D. Herold
41. (403) Joseph M. Robertson
42. (408) Wallace A. Scott
43. (420) Malcolm D. Stevenson
44. (449) George B. Moffat, Jr.
45. (450) William B. Cleary
46. (451) Ernst A. Steinhoff
47. (477) Robert F. Hupe
48. (478) Robert H. Fisher
49. (456) Lanier Frantz
50. (457) Robert L. Semans
51. (465) Leonard R. Boyd
52. (464) Donal H. Morgan, M.D.
53. (479) Bill F. Sparks
54. (480) Allen L. Leffler
55. (481) Robert L. Klemmedson
56. (482) Jerald D. Morris
57. (483) Joe Conn
58. (484) John M. Brittingham
59. (485) Carroll J. Klein
60. (486) David E. McNay
61. (487) Marion C. Cruce
62. (509) David M. Nees
63. (493) Elemer Katinszky
64.[1] ( ) Walter B. Cannon
65.[1] ( ) Charles E. Kohls
66.[1] ( ) George E. Coder, Jr.

Soaring

[1] International numbers not yet assigned at press time.
The non-consecutive inconsistency of international numbers is due to mailing delays and communication lags between the offices of S.S.A. and F.A.I.
* *Deceased*
Swiss Diamond No. 2, (42), Othmar Schwarzenberger
German Diamond No. 1, (23), Joachim Kuettner
German, (356), Hasso Richard Jauch
Hungarian, (   ), Sandor A. Aldott

THE SMITHSONIAN PLAQUE

Appendix II

GLOSSARY

AILERONS—Hinged movable surfaces at the outboard, trailing edge of the wings, arranged so when one goes down the other goes up, for controlling bank.

AIRSPEED—Speed of an aircraft through the air. In a level flight, no-wind condition, airspeed and groundspeed (speed over the ground) are the same. Flying straight upwind, airspeed minus windspeed equals groundspeed; straight downwind, airspeed *plus* windspeed equals groundspeed.

ANVIL—The spread-out, cirriform, ice crystal top of a cumulonimbus cloud which, after it has blown downwind from the generating mass, often looks like the overhanging end of an anvil. Indicates the cloud has passed its development stage.

ASL—Above sea level. Also termed MSL, meaning above average or mean sea level.

AT—Above terrain.

BASE or BASE LEG—Second part of a pattern approach to landing. The pilot turns crosswind, flying a course perpendicular to the strip, far enough away from the downwind end to make the turn onto final approach.

CIRRUS—High, ice crystal cloud, usually in the altitude range of 30,000 to 40,000 feet above the surface of the earth.

CLEAN—Streamlined and presenting few unnecessary obstructions to airflow. An airliner taking off is said to be "cleaned up" when it gets the landing gear retracted and the flaps up in flying position.

CLOUDBASE—The bottom of cumulus cloud, which appears flat in the distance, and marks the condensation point of rising water vapor.

CLOUDSTREET—A series of cumulus clouds lined up in a row, under which a sailplane can be flown straight, often at high speed, without the necessity of circling to maintain altitude.

CRABBING—When flying crosswind a pilot counteracts drift by crabbing, or nosing into the wind, enough to maintain a desired track over the ground.

CUMULONIMBUS—Towering cumulus which has developed to the point where it is dropping rain. Generally has lightning, thunder, hail, and other theatrical effects. Some violent clouds of this type make tornadoes. Often called Thunderhead by tourists.

CUMULUS—Any of the series of clouds having vertical development, as opposed to stratiform sheet cloud.

176

DEAD AIR—Air without vertical motion.

DOWNWIND LEG—The first part of a pattern approach to a landing. The aircraft flies in the same direction as the wind, parallel to the landing strip, and some distance to one side.

DUST DEVIL—A whirlwind that picks up dust, leaves, papers, etc. and points out the base and beginning of a thermal.

ELEVATORS—Movable part of the horizontal tail feather which controls up and down motion of the aircraft in flight.

FINAL or FINAL APPROACH—Last part of a pattern landing approach. The pilot turns toward the end of a strip from base leg, lining up with the runway and planning his descent so he will touch ground not far beyond the approach end.

FLYING SPEED—Minimum airspeed necessary for the wings to support flight.

FPM or M/S—Feet per minute, or meters per second. Can be applied to vertical motion of air, but usually to the sailplane.

FUSELAGE—The body of an aircraft; includes the cockpit and passenger or cargo area; not the wings, landing gear or tail control surfaces.

G FORCE—Gravity force. A man standing on the ground is exposed to 1 G, one gravity force. If he weighs 200 pounds and gets on a scale, it will indicate 200 pounds. In an aircraft making a turn or pulling out of a dive, his effective weight is increased by centrifugal force. If the effective weight is 600 pounds, the man is being exposed to 3 G's, three times the force of gravity. If it goes up to 1000 pounds, he is exposed to 5 G's. In sitting position a few seconds of this drains blood from the brain and causes blackout, which if continued will cause unconsciousness—an inconvenient thing when flying alone.

Many modern sailplanes are "stressed" or built to stand more than 10 G's before they break up. This is far stronger than most power planes or airliners.

GLIDE—To fly forward through the air while losing altitude; the aeronautical equivalent of sledding.

GLIDE ANGLE—The angle at which an aircraft approaches the earth under various conditions of flight. If a sailplane has a maximum glide angle of 30 to 1, from the height of one mile it can land thirty miles away in any direction; assuming level terrain, dead air, and no wind.

GLIDER—An aircraft made for either gliding or soaring. A term sometimes used interchangeably with sailplane; however, the troop carrying gliders of World War II were certainly not built for soaring.

Soaring

GREAT CIRCLE—Any line passing around the surface of the earth at a position of its greatest diameter, like the equator or a meridian of longitude. A great circle course is the shortest distance between any two points along the surface of the earth, although not necessarily the most advantageous for either sailing or soaring, due to the effects of ocean currents, winds or terrain features.

LENTICULAR or WAVE CLOUD—The wing-shaped cloud, marking a wave disturbance in the atmosphere, with edges which are incredibly soft and lovely to the eye. In the case of an orographic or mountain wave the cloud stands still above the earth at a position downwind from a mountainside. Moist air is thrust aloft by wave action past condensation point which is marked by the leading edge of the cloud. The crest of the wave is the deepest part of the cloud. On the descending, downwind half of the wave the moisture evaporates when it has gone down once again to the condensation point. This phenomenon may be compared to a waterfall which is stationary in relation to the earth, but formed by moving water.

LIFT—Upward motion of the air.

MAXIMUM GLIDE—The flattest possible angle of a sailplane's glide; or the speed at which this is obtained.

MINIMUM SINK—The speed at which a sailplane has the lowest sinking rate. Usually a little slower than maximum glide speed.

PENETRATION—Capacity for making forward progress through the air at little expense of altitude.

RIDGE SOAR—To maintain flight by using the upcurrent on the windward side of a ridge, cliff, or mountain. Most early soaring was done this way; hence the inevitable question: "Does it take much wind to keep them things up in the air?" When wind stops the upcurrent stops and the sailplanes come down.

RUDDER—Controls left and right movements of the ship. Actuated by rudder pedals under the feet.

SAILPILOT—Soaring pilot. Sailplane pilot.

SAILPLANE—An aircraft specifically designed and built for soaring.

SINK—Downward motion of the air.

SOAR—To fly a heavier-than-air craft without engine power, flight being sustained by upcurrents in the air. To gain altitude in a sailplane.

SPIN—A stalled maneuver in which the aircraft spins downward, turning rapidly but never picking up dangerous speed.

SPIRAL DIVE—A maneuver, occurring accidentally in blind flight, in which the aircraft begins a turn; the nose gradually drops and speed builds up. The pilot pulls back stick pressure to reduce the speed, but only succeeds in tightening his turn. If not corrected, wings generally break off the aircraft.

SPOILERS—Hinged panels, usually on the upper surface of wings, which decrease lift and increase drag when opened—for controlling glide-angle of a sailplane in landing.

STABLE AIR—Air without any vertical motion.

STALL—A condition in which airflow over the wing becomes turbulent and sufficiently disturbed that the wing loses lift, causing the aircraft to fall. Usually caused from lack of flying speed.

STICK—The main control in the cockpit. Actuates the elevators and ailerons.

THERMAL—A bubble or comparatively small mass of rising heated air. Some thermals are too small to keep a sailplane aloft but can be successfully worked by soaring birds; others contain more than a cubic mile of air.

THERMAL SOAR—To soar, usually by circling, in rising bubbles or masses of heated air. Thermal soaring requires atmospheric instability but is independent of wind and terrain. Most present day soaring is done in thermals.

THERMAL STRENGTH—The speed at which air in a thermal is rising. Depending on velocity, thermals are called "strong" or "weak" by pilots. Generally thermal strength is expressed in meters per second, or hundreds of feet per minute.

TOWPLANE or TUG—A power plane with a towrope hook affixed, capable of towing a sailplane into the air for launching a flight.

VERTIGO—Dizziness, panic and nausea caused by spatial disorientation in flight. Sometimes vertigo occurs from the misinterpretation of visual signals to the brain during night flight; but it much more commonly happens during instrumen flight when signals given to the brain by the inner ear disagree with those reported by visual observations of the flight attitude instruments.

WAVE SOAR—To soar upwind, gaining altitude in the rising side of an atmospheric wave or mountain wave. The world altitude record was made this way at Mojave, California. The sailplane got over 46,000 feet high.

YARN YAW INDICATOR—A short piece of yarn taped onto the canopy, which during flight gives a constant indication of whether the aircraft is flying straight or with yaw.

YAW—Flying at an angle through the air instead of straight. Done either purposely or accidentally this increases the fuselage

Soaring

area which is presented to the oncoming air and increases drag.

ZERO SINK—Upward motion in the air which exactly equals the minimum sinking rate of a sailplane. When flying at zero sink there is neither gain or loss of altitude.

Appendix III

INSTRUMENTS

As explained in the first chapter, the one indispensable instrument for soaring flight is the variometer, a highly sensitive rate-of-climb indicator which approaches instantaneous reaction speed. Unlike those of soaring birds, human senses are not acute enough to judge climb with sufficient rapidity for more than very crude soaring. The variometer makes up for this deficiency.

Next in order of importance is the airspeed indicator, a standard aircraft instrument. This helps a pilot control speed in the sensitive area just above the stall when he is circling to gain altitude. Sound effects make a fairly reliable substitute if this instrument goes out from icing or any other cause.

The altimeter is third in importance. A standard barometric aircraft instrument for giving height information, it is very helpful on long cross-country flights in which the terrain you are soaring over changes altitude.

All other instruments can be regarded more or less as luxuries.

Two instrument terms ought to be explained:

Redline: An actual red line painted on an instrument, indicating the end of safe operating limits. All aircraft have a redline speed (painted on the airspeed indicator). To fly at any greater speed would endanger the structure. Power planes have redline cylinder head temperatures, oil pressures, etc.

Pegged: When an instrument needle has risen to the peg, or stop, it can give no greater indication. Actual value in this case probably exceeds indicated value by an unknown amount. If an airspeed indicator is calibrated up to 150 miles per hour and the needle is on 150, it is pegged. Speed may be 150 miles per hour or greatly in excess of it.

The photograph on page 183 shows the instrument panel of *Cirro-Q*, typical of a high-performance sailplane.

1. *Aircraft clock*. The time indicated is four minutes before eleven. The roughened crystal rim controls a pointer, aimed at twelve in the photograph. This is useful for marking the time when a check point is passed. The center knob controls the thermal-timer needle, pointed at eight thirty in the picture. The second hand points at nine fifteen. Knob at lower left, just outside the eight, is for winding and setting.

2. *Electric turn-and-bank indicator*. The needle indicates straight flight or turn when flying blind. The ball in the level device indicates coordination, or lack of it.

3. *Oxygen flow indicator*. Blinks like an eye when a breath of oxygen is taken.

181

4. *Sensitive Altimeter.* Indicates in hundreds and thousands of feet, up to twenty thousand feet. Lack of engine vibration induces friction lag in sailplane altimeters. To get an accurate reading at any moment during rapid climb or descent the sailpilot will tap the instrument panel sharply with his fingertips, causing artificial vibration which lets the instrument adjust.

5. *Air Speed Indicator.*

6. *Cosim Variometer.* When the red pellet is up (left tube), the aircraft is sinking at various rates, ½ foot a second, then progressively 1, 2, 3, 5, 10, and 20 feet per second. The green pellet in the right tube indicates lift in the same amounts. When one pellet is up the other is always down.

7. *Memphis Variometer.* Calibrated in hundreds of feet per minute.

8. *Kollsman Direction Indicator or Compass.* The parallel bars outside the arrow pointer can be turned to your course direction. Simplifies turning on course after circling in a thermal where it is possible to get disoriented.

9. *Spoiler Handle.* In the 1-23D it sets the brake also.

10. *Air Vent.* Pull to open. Push in to close. This resembles an ash tray when open. A flexible tube leads to the nose of the aircraft for fresh air.

11. *Towrope Release Knob* painted bright red for high visibility.

12. *Switch* to turn on the electric turn-and-bank indicator.

13. *Accelerometer.* Registers G Force on the structure in turbulent conditions. The outer needles will stay at their greatest indication until a knob is pushed which lets them return to zero.

14. *Instrument position* for standby electric turn-and-bank indicator.

15. *Trim Control.* Set in one position for high speed flight; in another for slow circling flight.

16. *Barograph.* Not shown in the photograph, and generally mounted aft of the pilot. A recording barometer, calibrated in altitude instead of pressure. Soaring barographs, capable of being sealed, verify altitude, altitude gained, and the fact that a sailplane was continuously aloft on any given flight.

THE SCHWEIZER 1-23 D

Cirro-Q is a Schweizer 1-23D: (1 in Schweizer designations means single place; 23 means it is the twenty-third type built by the Company; D is for the fourth model of this basic type). The 1-23D is a single seat, high performance, all metal sailplane with a midwing cantilever monoplane wing. Its empty weight is about 515 pounds, including the instruments and oxygen gear. Its aspect ratio, the ratio of the average width to the length of a wing, is 16 to 1; maximum glide angle, about 30 to 1; minimum sink, 2 feet per second. It is built to stand over a 10 G load before breaking up; has a wingspan a little under 50 feet; length slightly over 20 feet. It is extremely crashworthy.

Schweizer sailplanes are famous around the world for this attribute. There have been cases in which these aircraft have taken frightful blows that reduced the structure to junk, but the pilot walked away uninjured.

Instrument Panel in Cirro-Q

Appendix V

WORLD SOARING CHAMPIONS

Date	Champion	Nationality	Contest Location
1937	Heini Dittmar	German	Germany
1948	Per Axel Persson	Swedish	Switzerland
1950	Billy Nilsson	Swedish	Sweden
1952	Philip A. Wills	English	Spain
1954	Gerard Pierre	French	England
1956	Paul B. MacCready, Jr.	American	France
1958	Ernst-Gunther Hasse	German	Poland
1960	Rudolfo Hossinger	Argentinean	Germany
1963	Edward Makula	Polish	Argentina
1965	Jan Wroblewski	Polish	England

NATIONAL SOARING CHAMPIONS

1930	Albert Hastings
1931	Albert Hastings
1932	J. K. O'Meara
1933	Stanley Smith
1934	Richard du Pont
1935	Richard du Pont
1936	Chester Decker
1937	Richard du Pont
1938	Emil Lehecka
1939	Chester Decker
1940	John Robinson
1941	John Robinson
1942	No Contest
1943	No Contest
1944	No Contest
1945	No Contest
1946	John Robinson
1947	Richard Comey
1948	Paul B. MacCready, Jr.
1949	Paul B. MacCready, Jr.
1950	Richard H. Johnson
1951	Richard H. Johnson
1952	Richard H. Johnson
1953	Paul B. MacCready, Jr.
1954	Richard H. Johnson
1955	Kempes Trager
1956	Lyle A. Maxey
1957	Stanley Smith
1958	Richard E. Schreder
1959	Richard H. Johnson
1960	Richard E. Schreder
1961	A. J. Smith
1962	John D. Ryan
1963	Richard H. Johnson
1964	Richard H. Johnson
1965	Dean Svec
1966	Richard E. Schreder

Appendix VII

SOARING RECORDS

In the American and World Records listed here there is no attempt to be complete. This is rather a listing of representative soaring records designed to show the steady and spectacular development of the sport through increasing performances in sailplanes.

Single Place Distance

World Records	American Records
1883, Aug. 28—John J. Montgomery (USA) Otay, Mesa, near San Diego. The World's first recorded successful glider flight—600 feet.	Same
1891 —Otto Lilienthal (Germany)—1312 feet.	
1902, Aug.—Wilbur Wright at Kitty Hawk, 2021 feet.	Same

This was the first of the Wright Brothers' soaring records which was to last for ten years.

World Records	American Records
1912, Oct.—H. Gutermuth (Germany) 2740 feet.	
1920, Apr.—W. Klemperer (Germany) 1.1 mile.	
1922, Aug.—Hentzen (Germany) 8.6 miles.	
1924, Oct.—Martens (Germany) 14 miles.	
1926, Aug.—Kegel (Germany) 35 miles.	
1926, Dec.—Gattaneo (Italy) 44 miles.	
1930, Aug.—Kronfeld (Germany) 103 miles.	
1931, July—Groenhoff (Germany) 137 miles.	
	1932—O'Meara—66 miles
1933, June—Riedel (Germany) 143 miles.	
	1933, Sept. du Pont—122 miles.
1934, June 25—du Pont (USA) 158 miles.	Same

An example of the heartbreak of record soaring. The great du Pont held his world record only one month and a day.

World Records	American Records
1934, July 26—Dittmar (Germany) 234 miles.	
1935, July 29—Oeltschner (Germany) 313 miles. (This was the first recorded flight to exceed Diamond Distance: 500 kilometers, or 310.7 miles)	
1937, May—Rastoronev (Russia) 405 miles.	
	1938, Apr.—Barringer— 212 miles.
	1939, June—Brown— 263 miles.

186

1939, July–Klepikova (Russia)
465.5 miles.

1940, July–Robinson–
290 miles.

These Distance Records held up for some time. Miss Klepikova held the Distance Record for twelve years. Mr. Robinson broke his own record seven years later. Flying out of Wichita Falls, Texas, he made the first American flight to exceed 500 kilometers. He landed after dark between telephone poles on an arrow-straight road in West Texas, after a flight which carried 325 miles.

Altitude Single Place

1891 –Lilienthal–(Germany) altitude
gain unknown.

1902 –Wright–(USA) altitude gain   Same
unknown.

1916, Sept.–Harth (Germany) between
33 and 49 feet gained.

1921, Sept.–Harth (Germany) between
231 and 265 feet gained.

1922, Aug.–Hentzen (Germany) 1137 feet.

1925, July–Auger (France) 2240 feet.

1929, Apr.–Nehring (Germany) 3868 feet.

1929, July–Kronfeld (Germany) 8320 feet.

1932, July–O'Meara–
4370 feet.

1934, Feb.–Dittmar (Germany)
14,137 feet.

1934, June–du Pont–
6223 feet.

1937, May–Steinig (Germany) 18,720
feet. (This was the first recorded
flight to exceed the present
Diamond Altitude gain requirement
of 5,000 meters, or 16,404 feet.)

1938, Nov.–Ziller (Germany) 22,434 feet.

1939, July–Stanley–
17,264 feet.

1943, July–Shelly Charles
–19,434 feet.

These World and U. S. Altitude Records were still good in 1946. By 1952, the Bishop Wave had been discovered and Americans had taken over the Altitude Records. The World single-place Altitude Record was set in late December, 1950, by William S.

187

Soaring

Ivans, Jr., who reached 42,100 feet. His altitude gain was 30,100 feet.

Duration Single Place

1883, Aug.—J. J. Montgomery (USA)   Same
Duration unknown.
1891 —Otto Lilienthal (Germany)
Duration unknown.
1902, Aug.—O. Wright at Kitty Hawk—   Same
26 sec.
1903, Jan.—O. Wright (USA)   Same
1 min. 12 sec.
1911, Oct.—O. Wright (USA)   Same
9 min. 45 sec.

It is interesting to note that the Wright Brothers, who are known to the world at large only for their powered flight, were international leaders in soaring. This Duration Record, which so greatly outclassed their earlier flights, was a big enough advance that it stayed a World Record for ten years.

1921, Aug.—Klemperer (Germany) 13 min.

Dr. Wolfgang Klemperer has lived in America for many years. He is one of the great and original creative brains the soaring world has produced.

1922, Aug.—Martens (Germany) 1 hr. 6 min.
1922, Oct.—Maneyrol (France) 3 hrs. 21 min.
1923, Jan.—Barbot (France) 8 hrs. 36 min.

During this brief period of only seventeen months, from August, 1921, to January, 1923, advanced sailpilots had learned the secret of long Duration flights.

1927, May—Schultz (Germany) 14 hrs. 7 min.
1931, Dec.—Cocke (USA) 21 hrs. 34 min.   Same
1933, Aug.—Schmidt (Germany) 36 hrs. 35 min.
1943, Sept.—Jachtmann (Germany)
55 hrs. 25 min.
1952, Apr.—Atger (France) 56 hrs. 15 min.

This record held and was listed in the 1955 Directory of the Soaring Society of America. After pilots were killed by going to sleep while trying to beat this record, the Federation Aeronautique Internationale wisely removed Duration as a record category since it had become a test of endurance rather than a soaring achievement. A comparatively recent flight was made in Hawaii, soaring in the ridge lift of the Pali, by a Hungarian Pilot and American Co-pilot in a Pratt-Read sailplane. They stayed aloft for 71 hours.

188

Goal and Return Single Place

1936, July—du Pont—
32 miles.

1938, Apr.—Straatman (Germany)
53 miles.

1938, June—Korator (Russia)
119 miles.

1938, July—Flinch (Germany)
191 miles.

1939, July—Kimelman (Russia)
212 miles.

1939, July—Decker
40 miles.

1952, Aug.—Coverdale (USA)   Same
260.34 miles.

1955, Sept.—Maxey (USA)   Same
310.7 miles. (500 kilometers)

Goal Single Place

1939, July—Savplov (Russia)
374.1 miles.

1951, Aug.—W. R. Wiberg
332.9 miles.

1953. June—Efimenko (Russia)
395 miles.

Distance Two Place

Two-place records in sailplanes were not recognized by the
F. A. I. until 1936. This explains the late date at which these records begin.

1936, July—Slatter- Bat-
terson—25 miles.

1936, Oct.—Iltchenko-Loguin (Russia)
83 miles.

1937, May—Iltchenko-Emerik (Russia)
253 miles.

1938, July—Kartachev-Savtzov (Russia)
384.6 miles.

1940 July—Stanley-E.
Schweizer, 219 miles.

1946, Sept.—R. H. Johnson
—R. A. Sparling—
309.7 miles.

1953, May—Iltchenko-Petchnikov
(Russia) 515.6 miles.

Altitude Two Place

1936, June—Slatter-Bat-
terson—5967 feet.

1937   May—Spilger-Hohenne (Germany)
7,283 feet.

1940,   Aug.—Barringer-Froehlich (USA)   Same
14,960 feet.

1952,   March—Edgar-Klieforth (USA)   Same
44,255 feet.

This flight has held another world record for over ten years.
In the Altitude Gained category, it set the record of 34,426 feet.

Duration Two Place

1936, July—Slatter-Burton
—8 hrs. 48 min.

1937,   July—Fox-Murray (England)
9 hrs. 48 min.

1938,   Sept.—Kahlbacker-Tauschegg
(Germany) 23 hrs. 41 min.

1938,   Dec.—Boedecker-Zander
(Germany) 50 hrs. 26 min.

1945, Nov.—P. Schweizer-
Hurtt—9 hrs. 17 min.

1951, Apr.—Arnold-Perl—
12 hrs. 3 min.

1954,   Apr.—Dauvin-Couston (France)
57 hrs. 10 min.

Goal and Return Two Place

1939,   July—Kartachev-Chechoulkine
(Russia) 212.5 miles.

1952,   Feb.—Dommisse-Barker (South
Africa) 270.9 miles.

1952, Aug.—Nelson-Perl—
153.9 miles.

Goal Two Place

1939,   Aug.—Kartachev-Grokeva (Russia)
245.4 miles.

1950, July—D. C. Johnson-
Fronius—223.14 miles.

1953   July—Popiel-Siemaszkiewicz
(Poland) 336.35 miles.

FEMININE RECORDS
Altitude Single Place

1938, Apr.—Jarleaud (France)
   3,848 feet.
1939, July—Zelenkova (Russia)
   6,795 feet.

1948, Apr.—Loufek—
   14,496 feet.

1951, Jan.—Gaudrey (France)
   25,414 feet.

Duration Single Place

1937 May—Modlibowska (Poland)
   24 hrs. 14 min.

1938, Sept.—Montgomery
   —7 hrs. 28 min.

1948, Nov.—Choisnet (France)
   35 hrs. 3 min.

Appendix VIII

WORLD SOARING RECORDS AND UNITED STATES RECORDS AS OF MARCH 21, 1967

(Under the new International Rules, to break a distance record it is necessary to exceed the previous record by 10 km., or 6.214 miles; speed records must be exceeded by 2 km.p.h., or 1.24 m. p. h.; new altitude records must show a 3 per cent increase over the previous record.)

RECORD CATEGORY	OPEN SINGLEPLACE		OPEN MULTIPLACE	
	WORLD RECORD	U. S. NATIONAL RECORD	WORLD RECORD	U. S. NATIONAL RECORD
Distance	647.17 mi. (1041.52 km.) U.S.A. Alvin H. Parker Sisu 1A 7-31-64	Same Odessa, Tex.	515.626 mi. (829.822 km.) U.S.S.R. Victor Iltchenko A-10 5-26-53	409.84 mi. (659.43 km.) E. Minghelli Prue Two-A 7-9-66 El Mirage, Cal.
Goal	520.55 mi. (837.75 km.) U.S.A. Wallace Scott Ka-6CR 7-23-64	Same Odessa, Tex.	436.66 mi. (702.744 km.) U.S.S.R. Pavel Antonov Blanik 4-24-64	248.073 mi. (399.240 km.) H. Hutchinson LK-10A 8-4-56 Grand Prairie, Tex.
Goal AND RETURN	453.98 mi. (730.62 km.) New Zealand S. H. Georgeson Slingsby Dart 1-6-65	348.24 mi. (560.42 km.) Sterling Starr 1-23D 7-15-61 Inyokern, Cal.	337.7 mi. (543.5 km.) Poland S. Ratusinski Bocian 7-29-62	234.660 mi. (377.660 km.) Harland Ross R-6 7-15-58 Odessa, Tex.
Altitude Gained	42,303 ft. (12,894 m.) U.S.A. Paul F. Bikle 1-23E 2-25-61	Same Lancaster, Cal.	34,426 ft. (10,493 m.) U.S.A. Laurence Edgar Pratt-Read 3-19-52	Same Bishop, Cal.
Absolute Altitude	46,267 ft. (14,102 m.) U.S.A. Paul F. Bikle 1-23E 2-25-61	Same Lancaster, Cal.	44,255 ft. (13,489 m.) U.S.A. Laurence Edgar Pratt-Read 3-19-52	Same Bishop, Cal.
Speed Over 100 Km Triangular Course	79.77 mph (128.38 kmph.) U.S.A. George Moffat, Jr. HP-8 8-16-62	Same El Mirage, Cal.	66.97 mph (107.78 kmph) Poland Stanislaw Kluk Bocian 9-2-64	59.36 mph (95.53 kmph) W. Briegleb 2-32 8-9-65 El Mirage, Cal.

Speed Over 300 Km. Triangular Course	74.48 mph (119.87 kmph) U.S.A. George Moffat, Jr. HP-8 8-6-64	Same Odessa, Tex.	57.515 mph (92.562 kmph) U.S.S.R. V. Tchouvikov KAI-19 8-1-64	51.169 mph (82.349 kmph) Harland Ross R-6 8-13-58 Odessa, Tex.
Speed Over 500 Km. Triangular Course	66.52 mph (107.12 kmph) South Africa E. Dommisse BJ-2 12-25-63	None established	52.00 mph (83.74 kmph) West Germany Helmut Sorg Ka-7 1-7-64	47.34 mph (76.17 kmph) P. Schweizer 2-32 7-29-66 Odessa, Tex.

	FEMININE SINGLEPLACE		FEMININE MULTIPLACE	
RECORD CATEGORY	**WORLD RECORD**	**U. S. NATIONAL RECORD**	**WORLD RECORD**	**U. S. NATIONAL RECORD**
Distance	465.532 mi. (749.203 km.) U.S.S.R. O. Klepikova Rot-Front 7 7-6-39	273.28 mi. (439.80 km.) Rose M. Licher 1-26 7-24-63 Sun Valley, Ida.	385.246 mi. (619.995 km.) U.S.S.R. Zinaida Solovey Blanik 6-27-64	170.316 mi. (274.100 km.) Betsy Woodward Pratt-Read 7-11-52 El Mirage, Cal.
Goal	391.46 mi. (630.00 km.) Poland Adela Dankowska Foka 7-7-64	226.57 mi (364.55 km.) Helen R. Dick Zugvogel III B 8-20-66 El Mirage, Cal.	385.246 mi. (619.995 km.) U.S.S.R. Zinaida Solovey Blanik 6-27-64	170.316 mi. (274.100 km.) Betsy Woodward Pratt-Read 7-11-52 El Mirage, Cal.
Goal And Return	283.96 mi. (457.00 km.) Poland Pelagia Majewska Foka 7-3-63	248.82 mi. (400.42 km.) Helen R. Dick Zugvogel III B 7-12-64 Inyokern, Cal.	260.54 mi. (419.30 km.) Poland Danuta Zachara Bocian 7-29-63	None established
Altitude Gained	29,918 ft. (9,119 m.) England Anne Burns Skylark 3 1-13-61	27,994 ft. (8,533 m.) Betsy Woodward Pratt-Read 4-14-55 Bishop, Cal.	23,805 ft. (7,256 m.) France D. Trouillard Wassmer WA-30 12-11-61	10,797 ft. (3,291 m.) Betsy Woodward TG-3A 4-7-50 El Mirage, Cal.
Absolute Altitude	39,993 ft. (12,190.20 m.) U.S.A. Betsy Woodward Pratt-Read 4-14-55	Same Bishop, Cal.	28,120 ft. (8,571 m.) France D. Trouillard Wassmer WA-30 12-11-61	None established
Speed Over 100 Km. Triangular Course	68.47 mph (110.17 kmph) South Africa Yvonne Leeman BJ-2 1-4-66	28.635 mph (46.084 kmph) Betsy Woodward BG-7 8-28-52 Grand Prairie, Tex.	55.08 mph (88.64 kmph) Poland Wiera Kaminska Bocian 7-19-65	None established

Soaring

Speed Over 300 Km. Triangular Course	65.98 mph (106.16 kmph) South Africa Yvonne Leeman BJ-2 1-14-66	None established	46.176 mph (74.314 kmph) U.S.S.R. Olga Manafova KAI-19 6-12-64	None established
Speed Over 500 Km. Triangular Course	64.16 mph (103.33 kmph) England Anne Burns Standard Austria 12-25-63	None established	None established	None established

TROPHIES AND AWARDS

(From: Trophies and Awards Handbook by Captain Ralph S. Barnaby, U. S. N., Retired Chairman S. S. A. Awards Committee)

1. *Lilienthal Medal*—The highest soaring award in the world is the Lilienthal Medal of the Federation Aeronautique Internationale. It is a perpetual award which was first made in 1938.

Established by the Federation Aeronautique Internationale in honor of Otto Lilienthal, pioneer glider experimenter and pilot, whose gliding experiments in Germany during the years 1890-1896 demonstrated that human flight was achievable, and furnished inspiration and encouragement to Wilbur and Orville Wright. Otto Lilienthal died in a gliding accident in 1896.

The Lilienthal Medal is made of silver and is 7.5 cm. in diameter. The obverse shows in bas-relief two birds in flight being captured by a man; the reverse bears a wreath and the words "Federation Aeronautique Internationale" surrounding a blank space on which the year and name of the recipient is engraved. A Lilienthal Medal is struck each year and becomes the permanent property of the winner.

As originally set up the medal was awarded to the glider pilot making the most outstanding gliding flight during the year in the opinion of the General Council of the FAI. In recent years the rules have been modified so that it may be awarded for outstanding contributions to the sport of motorless flight, not necessarily a single flight.

The rules for the award of the Lilienthal Medal now state:

"To reward a particularly remarkable sporting performance in gliding or eminent services over a long period of time on behalf of gliding, the FAI has struck a medal which is named the 'Lilienthal Medal' which may be awarded annually to a glider pilot who has either:

(a) broken an international record during the past year or,

(b) made a pioneer flight* during the past year or,

(c) who during a long period of time has given eminent services to gliding and is still an active glider pilot."

* The term "pioneer flight" is understood to mean a flight which has opened up new possibilities for gliding or has shown the way for fresh progress in the technique of gliding.

(It should be noted this medal is the soaring world's highest award; The World Championship is the highest competetive achievement in soaring. A very few, including Philip Wills of England and Paul MacCready of the United States have achieved both.)

Recipients:

1938	Taduesz Gora (Poland) for a goal flight of 557 kilometers.
1939-1947	No awards.
1948	Lieut. Per Axel Persson (Sweden) for an altitude flight of 8050 meters.
1949	John Robinson (USA) for his altitude flight to 10,210 meters absolute.
1950	William S. Ivans, Jr. (USA) for his altitude flight to 12,882 meters absolute; 9,174.5 meters gain.
1951	Madame Marcelle Choisnet-Gohard (France) for a duration flight of 28 hours 41 minutes.
1952	Charles Atge (France) for a duration flight of 56 hours, 15 minutes.
1953	Victor Iltchenko (USSR) for a straight-line distance flight of 829.8 kilometers.
1954	Philip Wills (Great Britain) for his outstanding services to the sport of soaring.
1955	Dr. Joachim Kuettner (West Germany) for his scientific work in soaring and his exploits as a soaring pilot.
1956	Dr. Paul B. MacCready, Jr. (USA) for his remarkable flying with which he won the World Championship.
1957	Luis Juez (Spain) for distinguished competition flying and his work for soaring in Spain.
1958	Wolf Hirth (Germany) for his great contributions to the development of the sport.
1959	Richard E. Schreder (USA) for three world soaring speed records for single-place sailplanes, in an aircraft he designed and built himself.
1960	Mrs. Pelagia Majewska (Poland) for the many outstanding soaring flights she has made including numerous world soaring records.

1961   Adolph Pirat Gehriger (Switzerland) for the many years during which he has been the active leader of C. V. S. M., the F. A. I. Gliding Committee.

1962   Paul F. Bikle (USA) for setting two World Altitude Records in one flight; 46,267 feet absolute, 42,303 feet gained.

1963   Heinz Huth (West Germany) for his unmatched success in German contest soaring and World Standard Class Championship competition.

1964   Alvin H. Parker (USA) for his World Distance Record Flight of 647.17 miles (1041.52 kilometers), Odessa, Texas-Kimball, Nebraska.

1965   Edward Makula (Poland) for his remarkable performances in World Championship Soaring which include a fifth place, a fourth, a third, and a first.

2. *Warren E. Eaton Memorial Trophy*—the highest soaring award in the United States is the Eaton Trophy. Awarded each year to a person who has made an outstanding contribution to the art, sport or science of Soaring Flight in the United States.

Perpetual—Established 1939.

Presented to the Soaring Society of America by Mrs. Genevieve Eaton, in memory of her husband, Warren E. Eaton, Founder and First President of The Soaring Society of America who died in a glider accident at Miami, Florida, on December 1, 1934.

The trophy is in the form of a tall vase type silver cup depicting in bas-relief soaring planes and clouds.

The Eaton Trophy is awarded each year to a person who in the opinion of the SSA Awards Committee and approved by the Board of Directors of The Soaring Society of America has made an outstanding contribution to the art, sport or science of soaring in the United States. While usually awarded to a person who has made his contribution during the previous calendar year, this is not mandatory and in certain instances the Board has gone back in years to pick up some outstanding person not before suitably recognized.

Recipients:

1939   Richard C. Du Pont
1940   Robert M. Stanley

1941	Floyd J. Sweet
1942	No award
1943	No award
1944	No award
1945	Ben Shupack (Awarded retroactively in 1956)
1946	Bernard L. Wiggin
1947	Paul E. Tuntland
1948	Fritz B. Compton
1949	Harland C. Ross and Robert F. Symons
1950	Paul B. MacCready, Jr.
1951	William S. Ivans, Jr.
1952	Jon D. Carsey
1953	Ernest and Paul Schweizer
1954	Ted Nelson
1955	Earl R. Southee
1956	R. E. Franklin
1957	William G. and Anne Briegleb
1958	No award
1959	E. J. Reeves
1960	Captain Ralph S. Barnaby
1961	Harner Selvidge
1962	Richard E. Schreder
1963	Dr. Wolfgang B. Klemperer (D)
1964	Paul F. Bikle
1965	John D. Ryan

3. *Richard C. du Pont Memorial Trophy*—Awarded to The U. S. National Soaring Champion.

Perpetual—Established 1947.

Presented to The Soaring Society of America by Allaire (Mrs. Richard C.) du Pont in memory of her husband, the 3rd President of The Soaring Society of America, and U. S. National Champion 1934, 1935 and 1937.

Richard C. du Pont, at the time a Special Assistant to General H. H. Arnold, Chief of the Army Air Forces in connection with the Army's glider program, was killed September 12, 1943, in the crash of an experimental miltary glider.

The trophy, symbolic of thermal soaring flight, consists of a bronze casting mounted on a mahogany base. It stands 24½ inches high overall and weighs 36 pounds.

The du Pont Trophy is awarded to the U. S. National Soaring Champion as determined at the U. S. Annual National Soaring Competitions. The trophy is perpetual in nature, and is passed along from Champion to Champion. The winners' names with dates are engraved on metal plates attached to the pedestal. In addition, each winner receives a bronze medallion bearing a bas-relief representation of the trophy for his permanent possession. With the trophy, Mrs. du Pont gave the Soaring Society 20 medallions.

This trophy succeeded the Edward E. Evans Trophy, the original National Championship trophy, presented by Edward S. Evans, early patron of soaring and founder of the National Glider Association under whose auspices the first two National Soaring Contests (1930 and 1931) were held. The Evans Trophy became the permanent property of John Robinson in 1946 when he won the National Championship three successive times (1940, 1941 and 1946:—There were no contests held during the war years 1942, 1943, 1944 and 1945.)

Recipients:

1947	Richard J. Comey
1948	Paul B. MacCready, Jr.
1949	Paul B. MacCready, Jr.
1950	Richard H. Johnson
1951	Richard H. Johnson
1952	Richard H. Johnson
1953	Paul B. MacCready, Jr.
1954	Richard H. Johnson
1955	Kempes Trager
1956	Lyle A. Maxey
1957	Stanley Smith
1958	Richard E. Schreder
1959	Richard H. Johnson
1960	Richard E. Schreder
1961	Andrew J. Smith
1962	John D. Ryan
1963	Richard H. Johnson
1964	Richard H. Johnson
1965	Dean Svec
1966	Richard E. Schreder

4. *Lewin B. Barringer Memorial Trophy*—Awarded to the pilot making the greatest straight line distance soaring flight during the calendar year, other than at the National Soaring Contest.

Originally presented to The Soaring Society of America by Lewin B. Barringer, in a provision in his will in which he provided for the trophy and laid down the requirements for winning it.

The Barringer Trophy is of modernistic design, in the form of an aluminum gull-type sailplane wing mounted atop a tall tapering wood column on a metal base. It stands 18 inches high with a wing span of 25 inches. It weighs 6 pounds.

Lewin Barringer was a former General Manager of The Soaring Society of America and holder of a World Gliding Distance Record made from an auto-towed launch. He was lost on January 24, 1942, during World War II, on a flight from the United States to North Africa, while serving as a Major in the Army Air Force in connection with glider acitvities.

Recipients:

1948	Donald H. Pollard (206 mi.)
1949	No award
1950	No award
1951	William C. Beuby (141.5 mi.)
1952	Paul F. Bikle (217 mi)
1953	Paul F. Bikle (202 mi.)
1954	Paul F. Bikle (249 mi.)
1955	Paul F. Bikle (280 mi)
1956	Paul F. Bikle (210 mi.)
1957	Sterling V. Starr (333 mi.)
1958	Julien J. Audette (236 mi)
1959	Harland C. Ross (365 mi.)
1960	Joseph C. Lincoln (455.5 mi)
1961	John D. Ryan (454 mi.)
1962	Harald W. Jensen (435 mi)
1963	Alvin H. Parker (487.24 mi.)
1964	Alvin H. Parker (647.17 mi.)
1965	Alvin H. Parker (370 mi.)

5. *Paul E. Tuntland Memorial Trophy*—Awarded to the person who during the preceding year is deemed to have made a soaring flight yielding the most scientific information recorded or written by the pilot.

Perpetual—Established 1950.

Presented to The Soaring Society of America by Paul Tuntland's family in memory of Paul Tuntland, an outstanding soaring pilot, whose work in the field of research, instruction, and competitive flying contributed greatly to the science and sport of soaring. Paul died as the result of a gliding accident, September 9, 1950.

The Trophy is in the form of a bronze plaque which is prepared each year from a master design and presented to the winner as his personal property. The plaque is 8 x 10 inches and weighs approximately two pounds. It bears the likeness of Paul Tuntland.

Recipients:

1951	Dr. August Raspet

1953	Dr. Joachim Kuettner
1954	Harold Klieforth
1955	Dr. Joachim Kuettner
1956	Dr. Paul B. MacCready, Jr.
1957	Stanley W. Smith
1958	No award
1959	Dewey J. Mancuso
1960	Harland C. Ross
1961	No award
1962	No award
1963	Paul F. Bikle
1964	Hans Zacher
1965	No award

6. *Helms Hall Soaring Hall of Fame*—Awarded to persons who achieve in a noteworthy manner in Soaring and to those who have made noteworthy contributions to the sport of Soaring.

Perpetual—Established 1954.

In 1954, the Helms Athletic Foundation decided that Soaring was a sport of such national and international stature as to rate recognition in the Helms Hall, the Foundation's International Sports Shrine. Accordingly, The Soaring Society of America was asked to select and recommend to the Foundation candidates for recognition in the Helms Hall Soaring Hall of Fame.

Recipients:

Ralph Stanley Barnaby
Lewin B. Barringer
William Hawley Bowlus
William G. Briegleb
Jay Buxton
Jon D. Carsey
Richard C. du Pont
Warren E. Eaton
Roswell E. Franklin
William E. Ivans, Jr.
Richard H. Johnson
Dr. Wolfgang B. Klemperer
Joseph C. Lincoln
Dr. Paul B. MacCready, Jr.
George B. Moffat, Jr.
John K. O'Meara
Alvin H. Parker

Raymon H. Parker
Irving O. Prue
Dr. August Raspet
John Robinson
Harland C. Ross
Richard E. Schreder
Arthur B. Schultz
Ernest Schweizer
Paul A. Schweizer
Wallace A. Scott
Stanley W. Smith
Floyd J. Sweet
Robert F. Symons
Paul E. Tuntland
Orville Wright
Wilbur Wright

Appendix X

PRESIDENTS OF THE SOARING SOCIETY OF AMERICA

The Soaring Society was formed in 1932 under the direction and leadership of Mr. Warren E. Eaton of Norwich, New York. It was the successor to an informal organization which had started in 1930 called the National Glider Association.

1932   Warren E. Eaton, New York
1933   Warren E. Eaton, New York
1934   Warren E. Eaton, New York
       Mr. Eaton died 12-1-34
1935   Ralph S. Barnaby, Pennsylvania, Lt. Commander, U.S.N.
1936   Ralph S. Barnaby, Pennsylvania, Lt. Commander, U.S.N.
1937   Richard C. du Pont, Delaware
       At this time the USA' had 8 Silver C pilots. (There was no Golden C designation at this time.) The U. S. distance record was 158.29 miles (du Pont). Mr. du Pont died 9-11-43.
1938   Richard C. du Pont, Delaware
1939   Richard C. du Pont, Delaware
1940   Earl R. Southee, Pennsylvania
       Mr. Southee was forced to resign early in 1940 in order to go into special service for the U. S. Government.
1940   Robert M. Stanley, New York
       Due to special government assignment, Mr. Stanley had to resign during the year.
1940   Ralph S. Barnaby, Pennsylvania, Commander, U.S.N.
1941   Ralph S. Barnaby, Pennsylvania, Commander, U.S.N.
1942   Parker Leonard, Connecticut
1943   Parker Leonard, Connecticut
1944   Parker Leonard, Connecticut
1945   Parker Leonard, Connecticut
1946   Ralph S. Barnaby, Pennsylvania, Captain, U.S.N.
1947   E. J. Reeves, Texas
1948   E. J. Reeves, Texas
1949   E. J. Reeves, Texas
1950   Jon D. Carsey, Texas
1951   Jon D. Carsey, Texas
1952   Jon. D. Carsey, Texas
1953   Jon D. Carsey, Texas
       Mr. Carsey died Sept. 6, 1962.
1954   Floyd J. Sweet, New York, Lt. Col. U.S.A.F.
1955   Floyd J. Sweet, New York, Lt. Col. U.S.A.F.
1956   Floyd J. Sweet, New York, Lt. Col. U.S.A.F.
1957   Paul A. Schweizer, New York

1958 Paul A. Schweizer, New York
1959 Dr. Harner Selvidge, California
1960 Dr. Harner Selvidge, California
1961 Paul F. Bikle, California
1962 Paul F. Bikle, California
1963 William S. Ivans, Jr., California
1964 William S. Ivans, Jr., California
1965 John D. Ryan, Arizona
1966 John D. Ryan, Arizona

Appendix XI

DIAMOND C AND GOLDEN C REQUIREMENTS

The Diamond C and Golden C awards are the highest badges given through the Federation Aeronautique Internationale, the controlling body of sporting aviation, to honor the accomplishment of fixed soaring tasks. The requirements are the same in every country and for all C awards a pilot must fly the ship by himself. For the Golden C, in addition to winning the lower Silver C, the sailpilot must make a flight of 300 kilometers (187 miles), and an altitude gain of 3000 meters (9840 feet) above low point of the flight after release from tow. The Diamond C requires a Distance flight of 500 kilometers (311 miles), a flight to a Goal announced before takeoff that is at least 300 kilometers away, and a climb of 5000 meters (16,404 feet).

* * *

These awards are won by men flying alone on quiet wings in the ever changing battlefield of the sky. They have known the terrors of rotor cloud, the crash of hail on metal, the growing of ice on leading edges and canopy, the near flash of lightening under a black overcast; and the agony of staying aloft in zero-sink, a few hundred feet over brutal terrain while the sweat runs and nerves pull taut. They have known the disappointments, the flights which almost came off, the near misses, the times when only one little factor made the weather wrong. They have also known the exaltation of the heights when, shivering from cold, with a heavy pull of oxygen through their mask, they have seen range after range of mountains growing fainter blue with distance, and over them blazing cumulus clouds towering toward heaven; they have circled with the hawk and have glided down at the end of a long day of soaring with knowledge that when the keel of their sailplane touched earth again it would touch beyond a magic circle on their chart, indicating a flight of 300 or 500 kilometers, and the glow of triumph overcame deadening fatigue.

These pilots have celebrated the wedding feast of man's beating heart, the slender wing, and the sky.

Joseph C. Lincoln

Bibliography

GENERAL WORKS

CHATTERTON, BRIGADIER GEORGE. *The Wings of Pegasus*. London, MacDonald, 1962.
The story of the Royal Glider Pilot Regiment in World War II dramatically written by its founder and commander.

GANN, ERNEST K. *Fate Is The Hunter*. New York: Simon & Shuster, 1961.
This book is not about soaring; but for those interested in the feel, mood, and smell of flying, Mr. Gann's book is a must.

GIBBS-SMITH, C. H. *Sir George Caley's Aeronautics 1796-1855*. London, Her Majesty's Stationery Office, 1962.
A distinguished and readable account of the scientific aeronautical achievements of one of aviation's greatest pioneers.

HORSLEY, TERENCE. *Soaring Flight*. New York: Current Books, A. A. Wyn, 1946.
An all-time classic of soaring, this book covers most of the field and is well illustrated with drawings, charts, and photographs.

IGGULDEN, JOHN. *The Clouded Sky*. New York, Macmillan Company, 1964.
The first full length novel in which soaring plays a major part. Run of the mill novel material; the soaring passages are excellent.

MILLER, RICHARD. *Soaring International Year Book 1965*. Los Angeles, California, Soaring International, 1965.
A distinguished sampling of writings and photographs about soaring by the Editor of *Soaring Magazine*.

MURCHIE, GUY. *Song Of The Sky*. Boston: Houghton Mifflin, 1954.
Possibly the greatest work of all time which is devoted to the sky, aircraft and flying. It would be difficult to exaggerate the magnitude of Mr. Murchie's achievement in this book which covers the whole field, including soaring.

ROSEBERRY, C. R. *The Challenging Skies*.
The colorful story of aviation's most exciting years 1919-1939, New York, Doubleday & Company, Inc. 1966. An excellent review of the development of aviation during the years between wars, with a chapter on soaring.

Soaring

SLINGSBY, F. N., H. C. N. GOODHART and others. *The Gliding Book*. London, Nicholas Kaye Ltd., 1965.
The latest English book written by a committee. Very interesting authors; marginal accuracy.

WELCH, ANN and GABOR DENES. *Go Gliding*. London, Faber and Faber, 1960.
A very good text and photographic introduction to soaring written for an English audience.

WELCH, ANN and LORNE. *The Story of Gliding*, London, John Murray, 1965.
An excellent readable history of soaring from the work of Leonardo da Vinci up to the 1,000 kilometer flight. One of the top books ever written on soaring.

WILLS, PHILIP A. *The Beauty Of Gliding*. London: Pitman, 1960.
A magnificent collection of black and white soaring photographs with an introductory essay by Philip Wills.

———. *On Being A Bird*. London: Max Parrish, 1953.
Mr. Wills is the outstanding figure in the English-speaking soaring world. This book describes his career from the time he began soaring until he became World Champion. Photographs and drawings contribute significantly to the text.

HANDBOOKS AND MANUALS

ASHKOUTI, JOSEPH. *Aircraft Mechanic's Pocket Manual*, 5th edition. New York, 1957.
The home constructor, builder, or shop mechanic will find this compendium of technical information most helpful.

FEDERAL AVIATION AGENCY. *Basic Glider Criteria Handbook*. Washington D.C.: U.S. Government Printing Office, 1961.
A technical book about glider construction, testing, and structure proving. A useful handbook for individual designers and craftsmen seeking information on federal airworthiness regulations for purposes of repair.

FUCHS, ALICE F. editor. *American Soaring Handbook*. Los Angeles: Soaring Society of America.
This handbook is still in process. The book brings together the leading American authorities writing on their specialties in soaring. To date, there are chapters on cross-country and wave soar-

ing, training, and aero-tow.

LUDLAM, FRANK H. and R. S. SCORER. *Cloud Study*, A Pictorial Guide. London: John Murray, (New York: Macmillan), 1958. A superb and instructive collection of cloud pictures with explanatory text. Some of the photographs are in color.

OSTIV (Organisation Scientifique et Technique Internationale du Vol a Voile.) *Federation Aeronautique Internationale OSTIV Division*, Paris, France. This book is an international directory of gliders. It contains perspective drawings, photographs, and three-view drawings of a remarkable number of sailplanes and gliders built since World War II. It also contains descriptions of the important pre-war sailplanes which are still flying. A considerable amount of technical data on the aircraft described is included. Text: English, German, French.

PIGGOTT, DEREK. *Gliding*, A Handbook on Soaring Flight. London: A & C Black, 1958. Although this handbook is directed mainly at students, it is a fine all-around book. Mr. Piggott is one of England's leading soaring instructors.

WALLINGTON, CHARLES E. *Meteorology For Glider Pilots*. London: (New York:) Pitman, 1961. A book on meteorology written specifically for the soaring pilot. This is the only book of its kind and is highly recommended for the serious student of soaring.

WELCH, ANN and others. *Soaring Pilot*. London: John Murray, 1955. (New York: Pitman, 1956.) This book is directed toward an English audience but is probably the best general instruction book on soaring. It is indispensible for students.

PERIODICAL

SOARING: The Journal of the Soaring Society of America. Richard Miller, Editor P. O. Box 66071 Los Angeles 66, California

Index

208

Soaring For Diamonds
has been set in Caledonia and Univers types
and printed on Warren's Olde Style by
Northland Press, Flagstaff, Arizona. It
was designed by John Anderson